Archaeology

Mark Dion
Archaeology

CONTENTS

Artist's Acknowledgements

It must be rare for any artist to find him or herself in the fortunate situation of being consistently surrounded by collaborators, supporters and assistants eager to share their clarity and precision with such energetic enthusiasm. Over the past decade I have been considerably lucky to have had the privilege of working with some exceptional talents from a wide variety of disciplines.

This book, *Archaeology*, is the consequence of the tenacity and vision of Alex Coles and Duncan McCorquodale. They approached the editing and production, respectively, of this volume undaunted by the many obstructions and irritations ahead. Without their conviction there would be no project.

I would like to thank the authors for their remarkable contributions: Jonathan Cotton, Emi Fontana, Colin Renfrew and Robert Williams. All excepted and excelled at the challenge of a deadline that would shrivel most writers' hearts.

The various projects represented between these covers result from the labour and good will of many friends and I hope those I forget to mention will forgive me. I'd like to thank Michel Ritter and Elaine Laubscher from Fri-Art, Centre D'Art Contemporain, Fribourg, Cecilia Galiena and Gordon Knox of Civitella Ranieri in Umbertide, The Nordic Pavilion, XLVII Biennale De Venezia, Jon-ove Steihaug (curator).

The acknowledgments for the Tate Thames Dig alone could easily fill a few pages. In addition to the volunteer team (Lloyd Amadi, Jean Briggs, Tom Chatterton, Robert Foot, Joan Godfrey, Alexis Holley, Gemma Hunter, Adbul Jalloh, Ahmed Jalloh, Bradlee Johnson, Mandy Kowaleuski, Marriott Lusengo, Gulcan Mahmut, Fahima Matin, Siva Meinerikandathevan, Beatrice Oluwa, Ruth Owoyemi, Jerome Perrins, Kelly Pratt, Hamsini Satachithananthan, Carmen Servais, Stace Smith) my friends at the Tate Gallery of Modern Art deserve a heartfelt thanks – Frances Morris (the curator), Sophie McKinlay and Phil Monk (project manager's with attitude), Caro Howell and Denise Ramzy (education and volunteers co-ordinators) and Adrian George (publicity expert). Although not pictured in this publication the Art Now project which is the final stage of the Tate Thames Dig has been curated by Sheena Wagstaff and Clarrie Wallis with the assistance of Rachel Meredith.

My galleries would be most irritated if I were to leave them out and not acknowledge the support they have given me and patience they have demonstrated. I would like to thank Colin De Land and the American Fine Arts Co., Galleria Christian Nagel, Galleria Emi Fontana, Galleria Georg Kargl, Cheryl Haines Gallery, Tanya Rumpff Gallery, and Marc Jancou and London Projects who have been instrumental in the realisation of this publication.

The fact that the work between these covers looks so remarkable is due to the excellence of the numerous skilled photographers who deserve special recognition – Andrew Cross, Andrew Dunkley, Eliane Laubscher, Rodney Tidnam, Mario Gorni and Jiulio Buono, and Simon Upton.

My deep appreciation and affection goes to my generous friends who have helped me work through the difficult aspects of the projects represented here. My particular thanks to: Naomi Beckwith, Iwona Blazwick, Alessandra Santarelli and Robert Williams. My dear friend and super assistant Lenka Clayton has earned a very special thanks for being such a major factor in the preservation of my mental health.

Lastly, my deepest gratitude I save for my partner J. Morgan Puett whose criticism, insight and intelligence influenced and enhanced all of the projects in this publication.

Tons of muck flows into the canals each day, and gives the crumbling back-quarters of Venice the peculiar stink – half drainage, half rotting stone – that so repels the queasy tourist, but gives the Venetian amateur a perverse and reluctant pleasure. Add to this the dust, vegetable peel, animal matter and ash that pours into every waterway, in defiance of the law, over the balconies and down the back-steps, and it is easy to conceive how thickly the canal-beds are coated with refuse. If you look down from a terrace when the tide is low, you can see an extraordinary variety of rubble and wreckage beneath the water, gleaming with spurious mystery through the green; and it is horrible to observe how squashily the poles go in, when a pile-driver begins its hammering in a canal.

JAN MORRIS, *VENICE*

IT MAY BE ART BUT IS IT ARCHAEOLOGY? SCIENCE AS ART AND ART AS SCIENCE

Tate Thames Dig: view of conservation and sorting at the tents on the Tate lawn. Photo: Tate Gallery of Modern Art.

... for the roses
Had the look of flowers that are looked at.[1]

Three tents on the front lawn of the Tate Gallery during August. Teams of volunteers washing, cleaning, sorting artefacts – shards of pottery, scraps of bone, bits of broken glass – all carefully collected by this same team of workers in the course of a programme of fieldwork, the Tate Thames Dig, on the foreshore of the Thames, first at Millbank (Tent A) then at Bankside (Tent B). In one of the tents Mark Dion is classifying the finds, in another conservation work is underway. One of the finds is a scrap of paper from a bottle bearing a message in Arabic script: paper conservators have made a beautiful job of drying, cleaning and restoring the delicate, damaged paper. In a few weeks the finds, suitably selected, processed, classified and labelled will go on display in glass showcases in the Gallery. It looks industrious, systematic – and it does provoke some questions. Can you call this archaeology? And when it comes to the Tate Gallery display – is it art?

Tate Thames Dig:
Dig Team on the foreshore, 1999.

THE PROJECT AS ARCHAEOLOGY

Mark Dion's selective displays, many of them in the field of natural history, are the result of meticulous processes of recovery, conservation, classification and installation. They are coherent, interesting, good to look at. Yet on closer examination they are not quite what they seem. Dion's work is plausible, persuasive. Everything in one of those natural history displays looks right – almost. But yet a nagging suspicion remains: is it the real thing? The uncertainty widens – how do you actually judge whether or not it is 'the real thing'? Indeed what is the real thing? And if this, which we see in front of us, is not the real thing, how different would it have to be to make the grade? What are the relevant criteria? These innocent paradoxical displays invite examination: they begin to pose questions. They lead us to ask again just what it is we do when we are doing archaeology or zoology or botany. If these are disciplines which classify and order for us the world in which we live, then may not such fundamental questions call into doubt the existing order of the world, or at least how we think about it?

The new work poses the same issues. Surely archaeology is what archaeologists do. They dig up the past, don't they? They undertake surface survey, carefully collecting and recording fragments of old things, and they put these in museum cases. Is not that what Dion is doing? But wait: something doesn't fit. Dion an archaeologist? He doesn't have the professional training. Is he an amateur archaeologist then, making a good go of looking like a professional?

Modern archaeology, I have to say, writing as a professional archaeologist, isn't quite like that. Archaeology may be defined as the study of the human past as inferred from the surviving material remains.[2] It is primarily about knowledge, information, and it depends mainly on stratigraphic excavation giving particular attention to the precise context from which each find comes. Finds associated together in a single stratigraphic context are likely to be contemporary – they may have been used together, buried together. From a study of these associations the archaeologist is able to make statements about the diet, technology, social life, even ways of thought of the people who used the things found. You can do that only to a limited extent from individual objects and fragments taken out of context. Gathering curiosities from the foreshore is really just beachcombing.

The epitome of military precision in the matter of stratigraphic excavation was achieved by Sir Mortimer Wheeler during his excavations in India in the days of colonial rule during the Second World War.[3] He was a pioneer of the meticulous systems for the recording of stratigraphic context which are still in use.

Of course, fifty years later, and in the post-colonial era, no-one today digs quite like Wheeler. But the objective of establishing context through stratigraphic excavation remains. That being said, however, Mark Dion is not only illustrating London's past with these finds from the foreshore. He is establishing, as excavating archaeologists do, a direct personal link with the past. The volunteers finding fragments of Roman or mediaeval pottery, which have lain there undisturbed for up to two thousand years, are discovering the power of that direct link with the past, that same immediacy which the archaeologist experiences on her first dig. Has this piece of Roman glass really been lying here for two thousand years, since some child in Roman times was scolded for breaking it? Does this piece of sheep's bone represent a family roast one evening in mediaeval Bankside?

Stratigraphy and context: the excavations of Sir Mortimer Wheeler at Arikamedu in 1946.

Does this bit of human bone come from the eroded cemetery of some Anglo-Saxon churchyard? These direct contacts with the past can be authentic experiences – these ancient fragments are all tokens of a life, of vitality in London's past, a past which you can hold in your hand today. Walking on the grey pebbles with Mark Dion in July – and on the foreshore everything is grey, it only takes on its own colour again when it is washed in the laboratory – it was easy to feel that London's past life is eroding out there on the grey foreshore. I was reminded of the last verse of Dylan Thomas's "A Refusal to Mourn the Death, by Fire, of a Child in London":

> Deep with the first dead lies London's daughter,
> Robed in the long friends,
> The grains beyond age, the dark veins of her mother.
> Secret by the unmourning water
> Of the riding Thames.
> After the first death, there is no other. [4]

"Secret by the unmourning water of
the riding Thames" – the grey foreshore.

View of the Tribuna degli Uffizi by Zoffany (1772): the Medici as Collectors.

DISPLAY: THE PROJECT AS ART

The work does indeed go much further than that of the beachcomber. For after the processing there comes the end product: the display. Mark Dion sets out to use the procedures of the archaeologist, and in some senses in doing so he becomes an archaeologist, even if archaeology today does go beyond these process of recovery, processing and display. The display cabinets which he creates would not raise an eyebrow in an archaeological museum, such as the Museum of London. They are authentic. But do we expect to see display cases in the Tate Gallery? Do they belong there? Another of Dion's subtly disquieting questions. Archaeology, we should remember was born of display, of the passion for collecting. Like Natural History it was born (or re-born) during the Renaissance, arising from the curiosity of the scholar and dilettante. The palace of the Renaissance prince would have a gallery of 'antique marbles' – Greek and Roman statuary representing the arts of the ancients – and a Cabinet of Curiosities containing a collection of curios, both natural and artificial. For example the Uffizi Palace in Florence, the home of the Medici, had its Tribuna, in which were exhibited the paintings of Raphael and Titian, but also their choicest marbles, the Medici Venus, Niobe and her daughters, the Dancing Faun, the Marsyas, the Apollino – all these famous works. This was the birthplace both of the Art Gallery and the Museum of Fine Art.

Its counterpart was the Cabinet of Curiosities. In such a Cabinet were all the wonders of the natural world, the exotic fish, the plants, reptiles (crocodiles were always popular): the Natural Curiosities, the naturalia. Such collections formed the starting point for the later systems of classification of the natural world, by genus and by species, as formalised by Linnaeus, and thus for the beginning of systematic botany, systematic zoology and so forth. These are the enterprises with which Mark Dion has already worked, repeating the experience of classification – mimicking the process almost – and recapturing some of the wonder of the early naturalists as they contemplated the natural world. One of the first attempts to grasp the living world in its totality and its variety was Aristotle's concept of the Great Chain of Being, which was so influential in the Middle Ages, right up to 1859 and Charles Darwin's Origin of Species. Along with the Natural Curiosities were the Artificial Curiosities, the artificiosa: statues, architectural fragments, metal objects, coins. These products of the arts of humankind included souvenirs from remote parts of the world, indeed the first ethnographic collections. They included prehistoric artefacts – flint arrowheads and axes, and bronze weapons.

Renaissance Cabinet of Curiosities: the Cabinet of Ferrante Imperato 1599.

As Mark Dion is very much aware, the division between natural and artificial underlies much museum classification today – it is a divide which, with the present exhibition he is resolutely crossing. If you go to Vienna to the spacious Maria-Theresien Platz, you find on one side the Naturhistorisches Museum and on the other the Kunsthistorisches Museum. The division is between nature and fine art – and the archaeological remains, the prehistory and ethnography often go with nature, just as in the earlier Cabinets of Curiosities. So the collections of prehistoric artefacts are found in the Naturhistorisches Museum. They do not make the grade as fine art. In New York, in just the same way, the 'Fine Art' goes into the Metropolitan Museum of Art, but the artefacts of the American Indian go into the American Museum of Natural History along with the rest of the ethnography and all the other natural history collections, the natural curiosities. Only recently, in response to the growing and fashionable enthusiasm for "primitive art", has ethnography begun to find a place among the fine art in the Met, in the Rockerfeller Wing opened a few years ago to contain it.

Hand axe, published by John Frere in *Archaeologia* in 1797.

Nor has the dividing line between artificial and natural curiosities always been easy to determine. During the Renaissance the chipped flint artefacts, the arrowhead, the hand axe of what we now call the palaeolithic period, were at first regarded as natural products, as thunderbolts. A hand axe, such as that published correctly as a prehistoric stone tool by John Frere in 1797 was regarded by the seventeenth century scholar Ulisses Aldrovandi, one of the great zoologists of the Renaissance period, as: "due to an admixture of a certain exhalation of thunder and lightning with metallic matter in dark clouds, which is coagulated by the circumfused moisture and coagulated into a mass (like flour with water) and subsequently indurated like a brick."[5] Matters of classification were by no means self-evident.

The British Museum, one of the first great national institutions which opened in 1753, at first contained both natural and artificial curiosities in just the same way as other early collections. They were separated in 1878 with the opening in South Kensington of the British Museum of Natural History, i.e. the Natural History Museum. In 1805 the British Museum acquired the Townley Marbles, the collection of the notable antiquarian Charles Townley, immortalised in a splendid portrait by Zoffany, which gives an admirable impression of the connoisseur in his study. The public museum display was more formal, but its origins in the taste of the discerning private collector were still evident.

Charles Townley's Library at 7 Park Street, Westminster by Zoffany (1781) with the "Townley Marbles", now in the British Museum.

Marcel Duchamp: *Bicycle Wheel* (1913), an early "readymade".

The early history of the museum is very relevant to the work of Mark Dion because in the course of his work he is re-creating and in a way re-defining the whole process of display. The development of the great museums established the convention for the public display of art: art is what you display in the Museum of Fine Art.

It was that enigmatic figure Marcel Duchamp who in 1913 highlighted the significance of the very action of putting a work on a plinth for display. A commonplace object – a bicycle wheel, a bottle rack, a urinal - was transformed into a "work of art" by the simple act of putting it on a pedestal and exhibiting it. Or at least that was the underlying logic of his action in exhibiting such "readymades".

Yet in retrospect what appeared at the time perhaps little more than an irreverent protest at the pretensions of the art market of the day has come to seem a very significant action. For that is how you establish what art is, in the visual arts: you put it on display. Duchamp was also one of the pioneers of the "installation work". He has been followed by others, by the display boxes of Joseph Cornell, the glass cases of Joseph Beuys, by the drug cabinets of Damien Hirst. One can situate the end product of Mark Dion's Tate Thames Dig in the display case in the Tate in the same tradition.

But as always with Dion, questions remain. For he, unlike Duchamp, puts into the glass case just what you might expect to see in such a case if you crossed the Park, as it were, from the Metropolitan Museum of Art to the American Museum of Natural History, crossed the Platz from the Kunsthistorisches to the Naturhistorisches Museum, crossed the Thames from the Tate Gallery to the Museum of London. If Dion, following Duchamp, can create "artworks" by placing artifacts – 'objets trouvés' rather than 'readymades' – into display cases, why aren't they still artworks when we see them in the Museum of London? Dion dissolves the boundaries.

ART AS PROCESS

For Mark Dion, moreover, the process of the work often seems more important than the end product, the artefact display. Dion is to a significant extent an archaeologist because he does archaeology, not because he puts Roman potshards in glass cases. He is a naturalist because he does botany or zoology, not because he exhibits butterflies. It is not really the end product which counts. The heart of the *Tate Thames Dig* is not really the display at the end of it. It is the work of the volunteers on the foreshore, and all that labour of conservation and classification in the tents. It is because they are doing archaeology, or at least what looks like archaeology, that the enterprise has a special fascination.

The analogy here is with the post-war generation of artists like Richard Long or Hamish Fulton for whom the activity in which they are engaged is what matters, not the end product. They may be described as process artists. For Long and for Fulton it is the activity of walking which is the essence of their work. The precise form taken by the permanent record of that process – a line of stones left in the landscape, a framed photograph in the art gallery, a word work printed upon paper and exhibited – is a secondary question.

Dion's project at the Tate sets the daily activity of the archaeologist, the collecting, the studying, right in the centre of the frame. He reminds us that the archaeologist, by placing a found object on display in a glass case, is himself highlighting that artefact, just as if it were a work of art. The observer today, the scientist, selects and isolates the object of study. That selection process, of course, is very much analogous to what happens in the Rockerfeller Wing of the Metropolitan Museum when ethnographic objects are promoted to the status of high art simply by being exhibited as such. Duchamp was right. And Dion goes further. He makes us uncertain where science ends and art begins, or indeed quite what the difference is.

Mark Dion: *Curiosity Cabinet for the Wexner Center for the Arts* (1996). Photo: Courtesy American Fine Arts Co., New York.

Anthropology, Mrs Herbert Fowler
Part of The Ladies' Field Club of York
Mark Dion & J. Morgan Puett, 1999

Paleontology, Mrs Herbert Fowler
Part of The Ladies' Field Club of York
Mark Dion & J. Morgan Puett, 1999

ART AS PLAY: ART AS COUNTERFEIT

Visual art from its earliest days has utilised techniques to create an imitation, a representation, a simulacrum, of the world. Mark Dion sometimes goes further than this in producing not just a painting or drawing which may be seen as a representation. He constructs instead an actual installation, a display of real objects – stuffed animals and birds, Roman potshards, mediaeval artifacts – towards re-creating the museum display. Such a display looks like the real thing because it is made up of elements which in some senses are the real thing: it is the result of a process which mimics in some respects the processes of the botanist or the zoologist or the archaeologist. Significantly perhaps he has entitled one of his most interesting exhibitions to date "Natural History and Other Fictions".

The work is playful, sometimes indeed witty, and the force of the wit lies in the meticulous and laborious precision which is employed. Huizinga in his illuminating work on play emphasised that play can be one of the most serious of human activities: "Civilisation is, in its earliest stages, played. It does not come from play... it arises in and as play and never leaves it."

One of the most frequent forms of play is imitation, mimicry. And when the original process is imitated with accuracy the end product is a counterfeit so effective that it comes close to the original. This is beautifully exemplified by Mark Dion and J. Morgan Puett's Ladies Field Club of York, a series of vignettes of an imaginary group of women amateur natural scientists from the nineteenth century. As examples we may take Miss Mary Buckmore representing 'Palaeontology', surrounded by fossils and carrying a formidable geologist's hammer, and Mrs. Herbert Fowler epitomising 'Anthropology', with her calipers for craniometric precision. The counterfeit is so meticulously produced, the rules of the game so carefully formulated and so scrupulously followed, that a slightly surreal authenticity results.

The Tate Thames Dig is likewise too thorough to be dismissed as mere counterfeit endeavour, too meticulous to be seen simply as play. It may not be archaeology quite as Sir Mortimer Wheeler would envisage it. But it does recapitulate the archaeological process. It subjects that process to scrutiny. It partakes in the immediacy of contact with the past through the material remains, the finds, which archaeology yields up. It puts it on display. It raises penetrating questions.

Objet trouvé: bicycle wheel on the Thames
at Bankside foreshore, 1999.

NOTES

1. Eliot, T.S., *Four Quartets*, London:
Faber and Faber, 1944.

2. Renfrew, C. and P. Bahn, *Archaeology,
Theories, Methods, Practice*, London:
Thames & Hudson, 1996, p. 11.

3. Wheeler, R.E.M., *Archeology from the
Earth*, Oxford: Clarendon Press, 1954.

4. Thomas, D., "A refusal to mourn the
death, by fire, of a child in London", *Deaths
and Entrances*, London: J.M. Dent & Sons,
1946, p. 8.

5. Daniel, G.E. and C. Renfrew, *The Idea
of Prehistory*, Edinburgh: Edinburgh
University Press,1988, pp. 29–30.

6. Dion, M., *Natural History and Other
Fictions, an Exhibition by Mark Dion*,
Birmingham: Ikon Gallery, 1997.

REFERENCES

Bailly, J.-C., *Duchamp*, London:
Art Data, 1986.

Corrin L.G., M. Kwon and N. Bryson,
Mark Dion, London: Phaidon, 1997.

Danaiel G.E. and C. Renfrew,
The Idea of Prehistory, Edinburgh:
Edinburgh University Press,1988.

Dion M., *Natural History and Other Fictions,
an Exhibition by Mark Dion*, Birmingham:
Ikon Gallery, 1997.

Dion M., *The Ladies Field Club of
York*, York: Impression Gallery, 1999.

Eliot T.S., *Four Quartets*, London: Faber
and Faber, 1944.

Haskell F. and N. Penny, *Taste and the
Antique*, New Haven: Yale University Press,
1981.

McShine K., *The Museum as Muse, Artists
Reflect*, New York: Museum of Modern Art,
1999.

Renfrew C. and P. Bahn, *Archaeology,
Theories, Methods, Practice*, London:
Thames and Hudson, 1996.

Schnapp A., *The Discovery of the Past*,
London: British Museum Press, 1996.

Thomas D., "A refusal to mourn the death,
by fire, of a child in London", *Deaths and
Entrances*, London: J.M. Dent & Sons,1946.

Wheeler R.E.M., *Archaeology from the
Earth*, Oxford: Clarendon Press, 1954.

Wilton A. and I. Bignamini, *Grand Tour,
the Lure of Italy in the Eighteenth Century*,
London: Tate Gallery, 1996.

THE EPIC ARCHAEOLOGICAL DIGS OF MARK DION

ALEX COLES

The personas of the artist Mark Dion are numerous. He is an explorer, a biochemist, an ornathologist, and an ethnographer. Over the past decade, by assuming one or more of these personas, Dion has constructed a number of installational tableaux inspired by his daring journeys deep into the jungles and rainforests of the Amazon; these projects have been widely discussed. In contrast, his four archaeological digs developed over the last three or four years follow a path distinct from the natural history series and have, as yet, received little attention.

The archeological digs are driven by a commitment to questioning traditional classificatory systems. Working alongside specialists from professional institutions, such as history museums and scientific research colleges allows Dion to blur the boundary between the official story that the professionals tell and the fictitious amateurish ones he stages. Throughout the digs, he assumes the museum's role of collecting, classifying and displaying. Each of these roles is played out in one of the three acts the dig is divided up into.

The first act is the actual dig, consisting of the excavation of detritus and ephemera from a selected site. The second is the cleaning and classification of the finds; while the third consists of the display of the items in a purpose built cabinet, a life-size walk through *Wunderkammer*. Carried through with an unrelenting sense of curiosity and cunning wit, the first two acts launch an assault on the audience's expectations. For with their provocative tactics, Dion's archeological digs are akin to a form of Brechtian epic theatre – hence the epic archeological dig.

DIGGING, DREDGING AND BEACHCOMBING

Because the audience is invited to each of the three acts of the dig, no one phase of the production of the work of art is privileged. Throughout the first two, Dion himself is equally on display – clad in either wellingtons and waterproofs for the dig, or white coat and gloves for the cleaning and initial classification of the detritus. By running these two acts together and then relating them to a third, Dion's archeological digs reveal the interdependence of site of production with site of consumption, eventually leading to the meltdown of the traditional boundary between the two.

History Trash Dig (1995) consisted of the removal of a two metre cube of earth from an area behind the city walls of Fribourg in Switzerland (used for centuries to tip refuse) and its transference to the Kunsthalle gallery where all the remnants of human activity were subjected to the archeological cataloguing process. The city's detritus, accumulated over hundreds of years, was cleaned, categorised, and displayed on the shelving installed around the gallery space. The final installation also consisted of a table of fragments of cleaned earthenware that could not fit onto the shelving and the remaining pile of earth from which it was extracted into which a shovel was sunk. *History Trash Scan* (1996) followed a similar process. On this occasion, however, all the detritus was removed from the base of a castle in Umbertide, Italy, and displayed on a number of makeshift tables.

Raiding Neptune's Vault: A Voyage to the Bottom of the Canals and Lagoon of Venice (1997/98) and the *Tate Thames Dig* (1999) differ from the above digs in that both lift their respective materials from the water and eventually display it in purpose-built cabinets. The former, commissioned by the Venice Biennale and later exhibited at Galleria Emi Fontana, is perhaps the most complex dig – beginning with the filling of a large container with dredge from Venice's canal. In the first of the following two acts, much of the dredge was sifted through and catalogued in front of an audience in a makeshift laboratory. The cleaned detritus, displayed on a system of shelving and in a number of treasure chests, was simultaneously exhibited with the laboratory in a parallel room. A year later, elements of the find were exhibited in a series of cabinets at Galleria Emi Fontana.

Tate Thames Dig, Lenka Clayton and Dig Team at Site II (Bankside), 1999.

The *Tate Thames Dig* pushes a number of the tactics
developed in *Raiding Neptune's Vault* even further by raising
a series of questions regarding site-specificity. The two sites
Dion selected on the Thames have a very particular
contemporary resonance: they are parallel to both the 'old'
Tate (Millbank) and the 'new' Tate (Bankside). In *Tate Thames
Dig* Dion foregrounds the dialogue between them in such a way
that goes beyond simply highlighting the relation between old
and new – a project that would surely work only as a publicity
stunt for the Tate. Indeed, by beachcombing the two sites for
both historical and contemporary flotsam and jetsam, Dion
cunningly inverts the key tactic used in the gentrification of
Southwark, namely, the repackaging of the past for present
consumption. The Tate's redevelopment of the disused
Bankside power station only adds to the process of gentrification
of Southwark which has been under way for some time, most
noticeably with the nearby Globe Theatre's recent renovation,
returning to its original splendour as a venue for open-air
theatre. Dion's provocative decision to repackage the past for
a contemporary audience while also presenting contemporary
material in both sites ensures that the *Tate Thames Dig* falls
short of merely presenting rare booty from a historic site for
a hungry audience to relish.

In transferring material from one site to another throughout the three acts of the dig, Dion recalls the Sites/Nonsites of Robert Smithson. And yet the way both artists deal with their respective sites could not be more different. Where Smithson indexes the earlier process-orientated stages of the work with a series of photographs and maps (that hang on the wall in front of the rubble taken from the site, which is exhibited in a metal bin), Dion displays each one with equal emphasis.[1] Nevertheless, they do share a fascination with mobile sites: Smithson with his transportation series from 1970 (including proposals such as *Barge of Sulphur Passing Through Panama Canal From East to West*) and Dion with his choice of the Thames – a river that almost enacts his anarchic process of overturning history in the way its turbulence continually churns up the detritus sitting on its riverbed and ebbs it along.[2]

Robert Smithson collecting obsidian for *Double Nonsite*, 1968. (Courtesy: Jon Webber Gallery).

CLEANING, CATALOGUING AND CONSERVING

The site where this act takes place is crucial to the dig. While in the first three digs the detritus and ephemera are catalogued in the same gallery space where they will eventually be displayed, in the *Tate Thames Dig* the cleaning takes place in a number of tents set up on the gallery's lawn. Lasting over two weeks, this act is the most interesting for a consideration of the role of the audience.[3]

The performative dimension to each of the digs, namely Dion's foregrounding both his and his assistants' actions, produces an aesthetic of interruption.[4] The experience of tactility invoked by the concept of interruption is also the organising principle behind Walter Benjamin's felicitous account of Bertolt Brecht's epic theatre of the early 1930s, the furnace in which the melting down of boundaries between actor and audience is notoriously under way.[5] Epic theatre induces the melting down of the boundary between actor and audience with the "filling-in of the orchestra pit."[6] The orchestra pit is filled in, as such, by the way the actors jolt the audience into participation – producing a connection between audience and stage that overcomes the gap traditionally inhabited by the orchestra. Provoked by this tactile experience, the audience "as a collective quickly feel impelled to take up an attitude" towards what they see. In other words, the audience is pressed into thinking for themselves.

Similarly, Dion's archeological digs meltdown spatial boundaries between the gallery and its surrounding context and those between artist and audience. Through their involvement, often taking the form of asking Dion and his assistants a series of questions about what they see, the audience of the epic archeological digs 'fill-in the orchestra pit', namely, the spatio-temporal boundaries between actors (artist and assistants) and audience. Dion's process of classification in the tents at the Tate is akin to a play of the epic theatre.[7] Dressed up in white coats as scientists and archaeologists, with magnifying glasses and small brushes for props, the actors fumble their way through a mound of detritus that takes centre stage.[8]

Dion's performance of the analysis of the detritus invites the audience to use the dialogic work as a platform. In Benjamin's words, this platform "does not merely transmit knowledge but actually engenders it" and so energises the audience into taking up their position. Most often this comes from the way the play, staged in the foreshore, the tents and later in the gallery, animates the audience and so provokes them into asking themselves a series of questions about what they see (both here and in history museums) instead of just passively accepting it as scientific 'truth'. With these tactics, Dion challenges the authoritative role assumed by specialists in order to reinstate more open possibilities.

Upon the platform, in this case a board propped up by two easels, the epic archaeology shakily unfolds. The scene in the tents is entropic: the mud and sludge traffics the assistants around the Tate's lawn, each of the fragments of clay and glass they fling makes a crash landing in its respective container, and at the centre of it all Dion is in the midst of a heated debate with a member of the audience. Meanwhile, the stench of the Thames coming from the discarded sludge intoxicates all – as producer, specimen, and audience meltdown and become part of an ongoing event that *is* the work of art.

Tate Thames Dig: view of conservation and sorting at the tents on the Tate lawn. Photo: Tate Gallery of Modern Art.

CABINETS OF CURIOUSITY

The final act of the dig is far more sober in prospect. Over the last four or five years, like the fieldwork and the cataloguing process, Dion has been gradually developing the cabinets of curiosity that take centre stage in this final act. They are a resting place for the detritus and ephemera that has been collected and catalogued during the dig.[9] (A separate body of work uses the cabinet exclusively, such as the recent *The Great Chain of Being* (1999) in the exhibition *The Museum as Muse* at the Museum of Modern Art in New York.)

The more recent cabinets are infinitely more complex than the earlier ones. Often double sided, they consist of a variety of shelves and drawers which are filled with the catalogued detritus and ephemera, usually organised and displayed in terms of the laws of formal resemblance rather than those of genealogy. The design of the cabinet not only reflects this critique of scientific laws of organisation (through spacing the shelving according to size of specimen) but also carries over the interactive quality characteristic of the earlier scenes in the project. Both the cabinets for *Raiding Neptune's Vault* and the *Tate Thames Dig* invite the audience to participate by opening its drawers so they can browse through the detritus and ephemera found there. In this way, something of the contemporaneity of the ephemera is retained. By contrast, the drawers of the cabinet for *The Great Chain of Being*, filled with 'dead' specimens, are sealed shut.

Mark Dion: *The Great Chain of Being*, Museum of Modern Art, 1999.
Photo: Courtesy American Fine Arts Co..

Raiding Neptune's Vault consisted of two hand-crafted cabinets and a number of pieces of shelving, each containing an assortment of different ephemera. In one of them, the artist's soiled lab-coat is hung next to his utensils. The Tate cabinet is a massive thirteen by nine feet and is divided, like the earlier stages, into two sections. However, a further scene is introduced into the final act of the Tate piece exhibited in the Art Now space: a series of photographs of the assistants. These photographs serve to further enhance the dialogue between artist, assistant, and audience. They also continue the questioning of the authorial role of the artist commenced in the earlier acts.

The absurd fictional museum collections of Marcel Broodthaers come to mind when thinking of Dion's Wunderkammers. Broodthaers's *Museum of Eagles* (1968–72), with its various departments, consisted of a collection of eagles on loan from various natural history, armoury, and war, museums. Each one of the eagles displayed in the glass cabinets and vitrines was provided with a label stating, "This is not a work of art." In his essay on Broodthaers, "This is Not a Museum of Art", Douglas Crimp intimately links his perception that Broodthaers is "an archaeologist of the present" to Benjamin's lucid discussion of the role of the collector. But while Crimp relies solely on Benjamin's essay "Eduard Fuchs, Collector and Historian" (1934), Benjamin was laying out the blueprints for his theory of the collector as early as the late 1920s. "In Praise of the Doll" (1930) includes the following reflection:

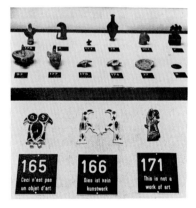

Marcel Broodthaers: *Musée d'Art Moderne, Départment des Aigles, Section des Figures*, 1972. (Courtesy: Maria Gilissen).

> The true passion of the collector is always anarchistic, destructive. For this is its dialectic: by loyalty to the thing, the individual thing, salvaged by him, he evokes an obstinate, subversive protest against the typical, the classifiable.[10]

Dion's anarchistic protest against the scientific techniques of archaeology is evident in the way he blasts the objects he collects out of traditional forms of classification. Where the collector, in Benjamin's terms, rescues things from commodity circulation, the detritus Dion retrieves has already been rendered outmoded. By cleaning, cataloguing, and displaying the detritus Dion catapults it towards a new life. It is as if Dion discreetly places a further label next to Broodthaers's, reading "This is Not Archaeology."

The fictional narrative piloted with the staging of the archeological dig and the cataloguing process as scenes akin to those from epic theatre is further pursued in this final act, with the *Wunderkammer*'s substituting for the performers, functioning as allegories of a pseudo-archaeology. But whether experiencing only the collections displayed in the cabinets, or the earlier acts too, each member of the audience is given the opportunity to fill in the orchestra pit and be an actor in the epic archeological digs of Mark Dion.

NOTES

1 The only exception to this rule is the display of *History Trash Dig* at London Projects in 1997. Here, on the wall behind the cabinet full of detritus and ephemera, was a photograph of the site in Fribourg, excavated two years earlier.

2 The use of the Thames contributes to the contemporary stage that discussions around site-specificity have come to, specifically regarding the notion of the mobile site. See James Meyer, "The Functional Site", *Documents* 7, Fall, 1996. Most of the interesting articles on, and interviews with, Dion have appeared in this New York based journal.

3 For a very different overview of this dig see my "Mark Dion: Tate Thames Dig", *Art & Text*, forthcoming.

4 Kwon, Miwon, "Unnatural Tendencies: Scientific Guises of Mark Dion", Natural History and Other Fictions, Birmingham: Ikon Gallery, 1997. Dion and his assistants replace the toys and stuffed animals that were the actors in much of the earlier work.

5 This mention of Benjamin should come as no surprise considering that much of the writing on Dion's tactics, and those of his generation, is underpinned with a discussion of his criticism from the early 1930s. See Hal Foster, "The Artist as Ethnographer", *The Return of the Real*, Cambridge: MIT Press, 1995. (For a critique of Foster's use of Benjamin see Renée Green's "Slippages", forthcoming, 1997.) Not surprisingly, some of the most interesting articles on the two artists that Dion is perhaps most in debt to from the late 1960s are also shot through with a discussion of Benjamin. See Craig Owens on Smithson, "Earthwords", *Beyond Recognition*, Berkeley: University of California Press, 1992, and Douglas Crimp on Broodthaers, "This is Not a Museum of Art", *On The Museums Ruins*, Cambridge: MIT Press, 1993. For Dion's interest in Benjamin see my interview with him in de-, dis-, ex-. Volume 3, *The Optic of Walter Benjamin*, London: Black Dog Publishing Limited, 1999.

6 Benjamin, Walter, "What is Epic Theatre?", *Understanding Brecht*, London: NLB/Verso, 1988, p. 22. Introductions to Benjamin's work on Brecht can be found in John McCole, "Benjamin and Weimar Modernism", *Walter Benjamin and the Antinomies of Tradition*, Ithaca: Cornell University Press, 1993, and Howard Caygill, "Speculative Critique: The Modern Epic", *Walter Benjamin: The Colour of Experience*, London: Routledge, 1997.

7 For further discussion of epic theatre and contemporary art, see Rosalyn Deutsche on Krzystof Wodiczko in "Homeless Projection and the Site of Urban Revitalisation", *Evictions*, Cambridge: MIT Press, 1996, p. 34. Also see Michael Taussig, "Montage", *Shamanism, Colonialism, and the Wild Man*, Chicago: University Press, 1987 and Dan Graham, "Dean Martin/Entertainment as Theatre", *Rock My Religion*, Cambridge: MIT Press, 1993.

8 A crucial part of epic theatre is the reinvention of both acting and narrative structure. As actors now become self-reflexive about their roles as actors, narrative structure is denied by the resulting emphasis on process. And so it is for Dion too. Yet Dion's intervention in the sites of production and consumption (with the digging and the cataloguing) as well as those of reproduction (with the museum installation in the final act) introduces a key annexation to the legacy of the productivist techniques of Benjamin and Brecht.

9 The two exceptions are *History Trash Dig* and *History Trash Scan* (although later the former piece re-emerged at London Projects in 1997 with a cabinet: see note 2).

10 This translation is taken from Esther Leslie's rich exegesis of Benjamin's theory of the collector in "Telescoping the Microscopic Object: Benjamin the Collector", *The Optic of Walter Benjamin*.

HISTORY
TRASH DIG

Approximately two cubic meters of soil and debris were removed
from the bottom of the gorge, just below the backs of the
sixteenth century houses boarding Fribourg's city centre. Over
hundreds of years, by device or accidents, people have thrown
material out the windows of these houses which has settled
in the gully. The removed material was brought to the Fri-Art
Kunsthalle's upper gallery and piled on top of a drop cloth
situated in the room's centre. Over a period of three days the
cone of dirt and remains were carefully examined and all of
the cultural material was separated. These human-made
items were cleaned, catalogued, numbered and placed on
a long shelf which lined the room. The first artefact removed
was numbered 001 and placed on the shelf, the next numbered
002 and placed next to it, and so on, until the shelf was filled.
The soil, tools, and cleaning apparatus were left in place in
the institution for the exhibition's duration.

MARK DION 1995

"View of dig site under row of houses",
History Trash Dig, 1995. Courtesy London Projects.

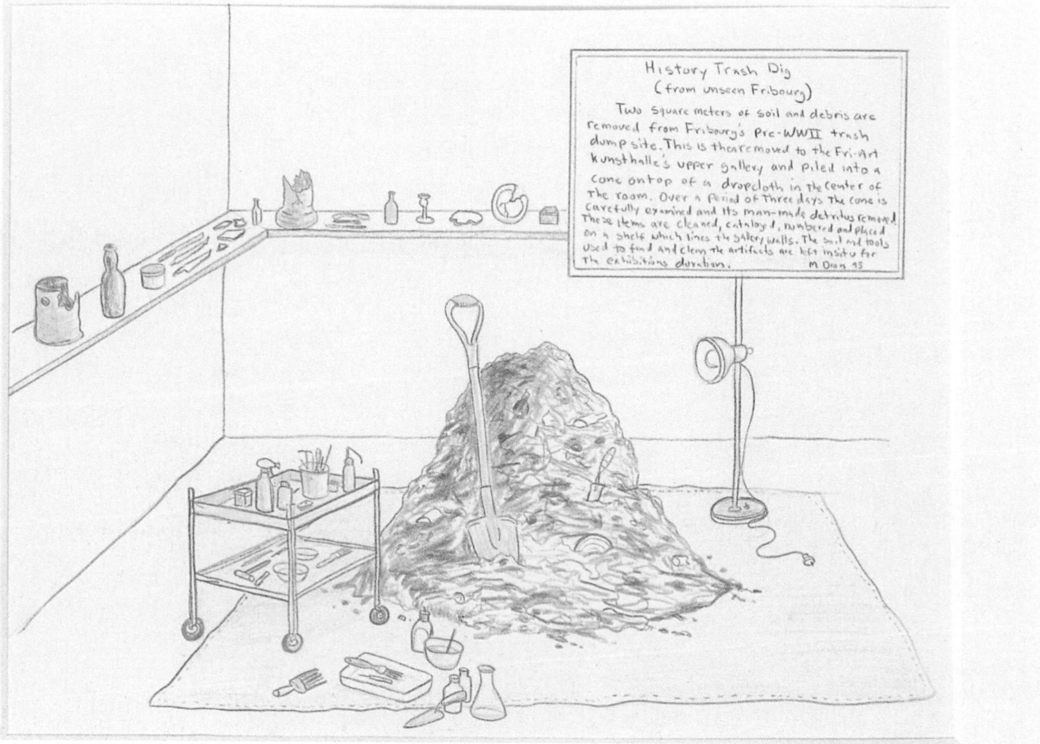
History Trash Dig
(from unseen Fribourg)
Two square meters of soil and debris are
removed from Fribourg's Pre-WWII trash
dump site. This is thearemoved to the Fri-Art
kunsthalle's upper gallery and piled into a
cone ontop of a dropcloth in the center of
the room. Over a period of three days the cone is
carefully examined and its man-made detritus removed.
These items are cleaned, cataloged, numbered and placed
on a shelf which lines the gallery walls. The soil and tools
used to find and clean the artifacts are left insitu for
the exhibitions duration.
M Dion 95

Mark Dion: *History Trash Dig*. 1995.

Mark Dion: *History Trash Dig*, 1995. Photo: Eliane Laubscher, FRI-ART.

Mark Dion: *History Trash Dig*, 1995. Photo: Eliane Laubscher, FRI-ART.

Mark Dion: *History Trash Dig*, 1997.
Courtesy London Projects.

Mark Dion: *History Trash Dig*, 1995. Photo: Eliane Laubscher, FRI-ART

Mark Dion: *History Trash Dig*, 1995.

History Trash Scan, installation detail, 1996. Courtesy Civitella Ranieri.

HISTORY
TRASH SCAN

The Civitella Ranieri Foundation is a remarkable residency program and workshop for artists of different disciplines and nations. Writers, composers and visual artists are housed and given superior studios in the fifteenth century castle or surrounding buildings located near Perugin, Italy.

   While there during the summer of 1996 I began to explore the forested slope behind the castle walls. Working one hour each day on a portion of eroded hillside I recovered an astonishing range of artifacts: bones, porcelain and stoneware shards, bits of hardware, fancy glass bottles, plastic bric-a-brac. Each rain would further erode my examination site causing a miniature avalanche of time. The material was removed to my studio and cleaned and displayed on tables for visitors. The objects functioned as markers for free-ranging discussions with other residents, visitors and the public. The material was later re-contextualised into a work which attempted to recapitulate the studio's ambiance of tentative procedures. The sculptural aspect of the project expresses the impression of the simultaneity of deep social history easily observable in the parade of architectural styles in many Italian cities.

MARK DION 1996

Mark Dion: *History Trash Scan*, installation view, 1996. Courtesy Galleria Emi Fontana.

History Trash Scan, installation detail, 1996. Courtesy Civitella Ranieri.

History Trash Scan, installation detail, 1996. Courtesy Civitella Ranieri.

RAIDING NEPTUNE'S VAULT: A VOYAGE TO THE BOTTOM OF THE CANALS AND LAGOON OF VENICE

Mark Dion: "Cabinet B", *Raiding Neptune's Vault*, 1997/98. Photo: Jiulio Buono.

LOOT

Mark Dion: "Treasure Chest (Relics
and Antiquity/Jewels/Precious Stones)",
Raiding Neptune's Vault, 1997/98.
Photo: Jiulio Buono.

I know I'm not the only one to think that Mark Dion's work has a lot to do with fiction. Its presence always seems to hover over his installations. Things, objects, and fragments take the place of people and do not hesitate to tell you their stories and their version of the facts. I have even noticed that his works emanate a special smell.

It was in the autumn and we were exhibiting *History Trash Scan* (*Civitella Ranieri*) when the cat started coming in. It was the tracks it left behind that made us notice its presence. On the gray vinyl surface of the 50s desk that we found in Torino, together with fragments neatly arranged, next to enameled zinc basins full of cleaning tools and a mandible bone whitened by centuries, were the little prints of the cat paws. It had walked through all this debris so delicately that not one of the fragile objects had been broken or moved. Even the magnifying glass had remained in its place. (Later on, I noticed that this was the object most desired by visitors of the human species.) I took the cat story as a premonition, a sign. Another, more noble, feline had probably already started spying on our moves and was keeping a close watch over the Amerikano. Furthermore, Civitella Ranieri (the place Mark was working in) recalled a Venetian style studio. I had always associated the meticulousness of Mark's working process with that of Vettore Carpaccio (meticulousness and a passion for cataloguing are considered as qualities peculiar to the Venetian type). Didn't that character, who had just stepped away form his research and obsessive cataloguing, look like a modern S. Jerome? Or maybe it was Paolo Sarpi the rebellious monk, Venetian doctor, researcher and philosopher, that he looked like.

When at the end of the summer, Maresciallo Canicola phoned to tell me Mr. Dion's work at the Venice Biennale, *Raiding Neptune's Vault: A Voyage to the Bottom of the Canals and Lagoon of Venice*, had been confiscated by the Nucleo Speciale dei Carabinieri per la Protezione del Patrimonio Artistico Nazionale, I was still basking in the compliments that Mark's work had received at the Biennale. So at this news I almost fainted.

I picked up the phone and tried to make some sense of the situation. The Maresciallo was kind: he explained that there had been an anonymous report informing them that Mr. Dion's work in the Northern Pavilion contained pieces of priceless archaeological value. Through my good connections in the field of archaeology (my brother is an archaeologist) I was able to discover that, yes, indeed, there was an Italian law passed during the Fascist era making it illegal to remove any materials taken from Italian soil (or water). I even called lawyers and notaries, all admirers and collectors of Mark's work, who took a sincere interest in his plight. At the end of this series of phone calls it became clear to me that I had to go to Venice to find out as much as I could from the Carabinieri. I made an appointment with the Maresciallo for the following morning.

Sleepy and worried, after having looked long and hard for the right clothes for a meeting with the military police, the next morning found me on the train from Milano Centrale station to Venezia Santa Lucia. My thoughts were running twice as fast as the intercity train. Why did this happen? Who could have done something like this? The idea of a plot took shape in my mind. Meanwhile, with half closed eyes, I was tossed here and there by the jolting movements of the train. The smoking chimney stacks of Mestre appeared out of nowhere, before Venice came into view through the Autumn mist. Venice, that whorish and treacherous city, the perennial domain of murder and intrigue.

American and Japanese tourists started making a noise on the train – excited at the sight of the Serenissima. And suddenly there I was – inside the postcard, immersed in the tepid September light: on a vaporetto heading for S. Marco.

Mark Dion: "Dredging Canal Rio della Sensa",
Raiding Neptune's Vault, 1997/98.

Obviously the offices of the Carabinieri in charge of the country's artistic patrimony were located in a beautiful palazzo overlooking the Piazza S. Marco. Obviously, the offices were on the top floor and obviously there was no elevator, only narrow stone stairs whose steps where worn away through use. Before ringing the bell I had to stop for a moment to catch my breath - I had run up the steps without realising it.

The Maresciallo was as kind in person as he had seemed over the phone and he proved to have some knowledge of art history which, in my eyes, immediately made him a more respectable interlocutor. However, he proceeded to say something that sent a chill up my spine. "Since Mr. Dion is an American citizen, and since the work is being exhibited in the Nordic Pavilion, we have a situation akin to the crime of illegal international art trafficking, imputable to both the artist and to you as his gallerist." As far as I was concerned, I thought the accusation an accurate description of my activity: afterall, international art trafficking did not sound too bad! But I restrained myself from saying anything in this regard. I tried to take a more rational approach and get to the bottom of things.

It had been an anonymous report in perfect Venetian style that had tipped them off. Had not the "Bocca del Leone" (Lion's Mouth) worked for centuries in Venice, and wasn't the counter where the anonymous accusations were made still visible? The Maresciallo patiently explained to me that they were obliged to investigate every report even when made anonymously. But then he came to my rescue by telling me that the case was under the jurisdiction of the Archaeological Inspector of the Belle Arti in Padua, Doctor Pedrazzon. He smiled again and gave me Pedrazzon's phone number. At least I had gotten something for my efforts. I bid him goodbye and took the vaporetto to the giardini. I had informed the administration of the Biennale that I was coming so I found a pass at the entrance.

I hurried towards the Northern Pavilion. There were still a few visitors wandering through the walkways of the giardini, but at the Pavilion I found only a gloomy Henrik Hakansson, the Swedish artist who had stayed behind to take care of his butterflies. He seemed shocked by what had happened. He told me that men in dark suits, accompanied by other men in uniform, had arrived one morning and had placed strange labels under Mark's work that read "these pieces are the property of the Italian State."

There was nothing left for me to do other than to acknowledge the facts and book a seat on the first train back to Milano. But first I would chase after doctor Pedrazzon. "Sorry, he is not here." And "Sorry, he has just left" was all I heard. But I finally managed to speak with him. During our phone conversation he was very reticent and clearly diffident. Things were not going well. I then spoke to my lawyers who advised me to resolve things in a friendly way because as far as the law was concerned we were at fault. How I hate Venice!

Mark Dion: "Dredging", *Raiding Neptune's Vault*, 1997/98.

I finally got my appointment with Pedrazzon. This time my appointment was at Palazzo Ducale, where the offices of the Sovrintendenza Archeologica are located. Doctor Pedrazzon looked very much at ease amid all those art treasures and so was I. Tall, and in his mid-40s, his beard and glasses made him look big and imposing. He immediately embarked upon a tirade against "those Americans, who come here thinking they can do whatever they want." To emphasise his point he rose and slammed his large hand against the desk. Maybe he wanted to frighten me. (I reflected on the fact that once the Venetians were lords and pirates of the seas.) At this point, clouds of dust rose from the piles of paper on his desk. There was dust everywhere. It is the patina of time I told myself, we are in Venice. On the other tables in his large office I saw plastic containers full of fragments – some labeled, some not. It looked like Mark's installation. Yet in his anti-American fanaticism I recognised the faded history of a 1968-styled communist. I'm a daughter of the same revolution from ten years later, so I lent forward and targeted my strategic plea. I started by emphasising the fact that not all Americans were alike. Following this I took out book after book, catalogue after catalogue, as if they were my weapons. Before he could even interrupt me I started to speak fervently about Mark's work. I talked non-stop for ten whole minutes, slipping dozens of coloured images under his eyes.

Then, as I swung into the second half of my impassioned plea
I could tell that he was softening up, that he liked the work, and
that he was intrigued. He had never thought that the cataloguing
of fragments could be considered as an artistic gesture. The
Amerikano was no longer an enemy, but rather the companion
of a summer excavation project perhaps, with whom to share
the passion for research. I felt I had succeeded, that we wouldn't
be dragged to court on "international smuggling" charges, and
that, above all else, the work would not be confiscated. But at
that very moment Pedrazzoa counter-attacked. Indeed, he liked
the work. But perhaps he liked it a little too much because now
he wanted one of the pieces. "Pardon me but I don't understand
doctor Pedrazzoa." "But it is quite clear" he replied. "First we
have to make another inspection, then you and the artist could
donate one of the pieces in question to the State of Italy."
(I found myself utterly incapable of measuring the importance
of the word "could.") "For example," he goes on, "those wooden
boxes with the fragments? Well, we have identified some rather
important material in it." I could not believe it! The treachorous
Venetian had already chosen the piece he wanted. If he had
had some other respectable source of income besides his State
salary, I would have turned him into a respectable collector
without further ado. But when all was said and done, the
proposal did seem rather acceptable to me. By the way, the
title of the piece that Pedrazzon had chosen was *Loot*.

Mark Dion: *Raiding Neptune's Vault*,
objects freshly removed from the dredged
muck, 1997/98. Photo: Mario Gorni

Raiding Neptune's Vault, plants and animals from the Lagoon of Venice, outside the Nordic Pavilion,1997/98. Photo: Mario Gorni.

LAST ACT, VENICE, 10 NOVEMBER 1997, 1:30 PM

November is my favourite month in Venice. On the occasion of this visit I do not show up alone but am accompanied by a photographer (naturally). Mario Gorni, a man who rises to every occasion, is the cameraman (he is otherwise known to be a gallerist at Cusano Milanino). This time the walkways of the Giardini are covered by a thick mantle of dry leaves that make crunching noises under our feet. There is an atmosphere of abandon. Pidgeons dominate the site. Maurizio's work at the Italian Pavilion suddenly seemed more meaningful to me. There was not a visitor in sight. As we reached the Northern Pavilion I wondered how Hakansson's butterflies were managing in the cold, they could all be dead.

Pedrazzon arrived in a bottle-green riding jacket and a blue felt cap. Clearly he was duly dressed to act in his professional capacity. He was also accompanied by a pleasant looking, but rather reserved woman, all bundled up in clothes. Dottoressa Picchio was an expert in pottery and also his assistant. They started their investigations. "Here we have, for example, a seventeenth-century graffita," Dottoressa Picchio said, indicating the incriminating piece. "Here is a fragment of Chinese porcelain, a majolica, an Islamic piece, a Sephardic fragment, another Chinese ceramic this time with a dragon. This piece is English, eighteenth-century I would say." she said, fumbling amongst others. "Ah, a cup from the Bar Sport café!" I exclaimed, indicating a fragment from an espresso coffee cup, no longer able to endure the weight of so much history. Mario's camera clicked away as he sped through another film. At this, the archaeologists' excitement grew (Pedrazzon had

Mark Dion: "Laboratory/Collection",
Raiding Neptune's Vault, 1997/98.
Photo: Julio Buono.

been immediately seduced by Mario's camera). They started wanting to see everything, touch everything. They even wanted to tear off the pieces in "Cabinet B" which were glued down. "Be careful or you'll break everything that way" I retorted. They needed some tools in order to examine the finds. No problem, one only need ask. Magnifying glass? Here it is (still in its place, untouched). After a while the archaeologists calmed down. The solemn moment had arrived for *Loot* to pass from my hands into the hands of the Italian State. I felt like Caterina Coronaro, Queen of Cyprus, when she gave up her crown to Venice. An act of renunciation. "It will be exhibited at Palazzo Ducale" Pedrazzon told me triumphantly. "I'll wrap it up for you" I answered obligingly.

So the next time you are in Venice take a tour of Palazzo Ducale. Among the Assyrian Chimeras, looted and transformed by the Venetians, the paintings by Tintoretto and Veronese, amid the banners ripped off Turkish ships by the Venetian fleet, you can now stop and admire Mark Dion's *Loot*.

Translated by Mila Dau

Mark Dion: "Laboratory/Collection", *Raiding Neptune's Vault*, 1997/98. Photo: Julio Buono. Courtesy Galleria Emi Fontana.

Mark Dion: "Laboratory/Collection", *Raiding Neptune's Vault*, detail, 1997/98. Photo: Julio Buono. Courtesy Galleria Emi Fontana.

Mark Dion: *Raiding Neptune's Vault*,
Nordic Pavilion, detail, 1997.

Mark Dion: "Laboratory/Collection",
Raiding Neptune's Vault, 1997/98.
Photo: Julio Buono. Courtesy Galleria
Emi Fontana.

Mark Dion: "Loot 2", *Raiding Neptune's Vault*, 1997/98.

BALLAST-HEAVERS AND BATTLE-AXES: THE 'GOLDEN AGE' OF THAMES FINDS

JONATHAN COTTON

Writing at the end of the 1920s, and very probably at the behest of Dr Mortimer Wheeler, George (G F) Lawrence, that "honest rogue," collector, dealer in antiquities and sometime agent of the London Museum, said that he feared 'the Golden Age' of Thames finds was past. There are good reasons for dating this Golden Age between the late 1820s and, say, the close of the century, as we shall see. Certainly, most of the major artefacts, like the life-size bronze head of Hadrian, the Battersea shield and the Waterloo Bridge helmet were retrieved during this period, and, more precisely, within its middle decades, though the information we have about their actual recovery is often remarkably, not to say suspiciously, slight. The same decades also witnessed the establishment of many of the national and county archaeological societies, the passing of the Museums Act and the first meaningful archaeological excavations within the London region.

The finds dredged from the Thames at this time are so spectacular and so seemingly well known that they have rarely attracted the sort of critical attention regularly afforded land finds, beyond that of the 'art historical' and gross distributional type. Thus no self-respecting distribution map of virtually any object class is complete without its quota of Thames finds. However, the work of the Thames Archaeological Survey (1995-1999) has had the beneficial and long overdue effect of re-focusing interest on the necessary minutiae of location and context, as several published papers have already made abundantly clear. In the second part of this essay we will look again, and in a similar 'archaeological' way, at parts of this mass of historic material to see whether further useful information can be extracted from it. But first it is necessary to sketch in the contemporary riparian and social context within which the material was accumulated.

RIPARIAN POLITICS

Firstly, let us look briefly at the various bodies who controlled the Thames, and the limits of their control. For centuries the river has been the subject of governmental regulation, with the over-riding concern being to ensure that it should be navigable and free from obstruction. Historically this has involved 1) the removal of upstanding obstructions, 2) programmes of dredging, and 3) the construction and maintenance of embankments. A succession of royal decrees, of charters including Magna Carta, petitions and, from 1350 onwards, Acts of Parliament, sought to ensure the clearance of fish-weirs, flash-locks, stakes and other hindrances – pronouncements which frequently brought riparian landholders and weir and mill owners into direct conflict with other river users.

Between 1197 and 1857 the tidal reaches of the river at least were under the jurisdiction of the Mayor and Corporation of the City of London, "strict as far westward as Staines, vague and doubtful beyond" as Fred Thacker puts it in his classic *Thames Highway*. The historic limits of the City's jurisdiction are today marked by a replica stone placed on the Middlesex bank upstream of Staines Bridge and inscribed 'God Save the City of London'. Following seventeen years of legal wrangling the Thames Conservancy was set up in 1857 and charged with the care of the Thames from Staines to the sea, thus depriving the City of its ancient powers and rights.

A further Act of 1866 consolidated and extended the Conservancy powers to the Upper Thames and, amongst other measures, abolished the ballastage monopoly. That is the right to ballast shipping in the Pool of London, exercised more or less continuously since 1594 by the Corporation of the Trinity House of Deptford Strand, a body established by Royal Charter in 1514 following a petition of 1513. In addition to supplying ballast, Trinity House was also responsible for providing river pilots and beacons. Ballastage is an issue crucial to our concerns here and one to which we will shortly return.

The Official Port of
London Boundary Stone

In their turn, Conservancy operations were restricted to the
non-tidal river in 1909 with the creation of the Port of London
Authority, which was granted control over the tidal river
between Teddington Lock and Yantlet Creek near the mouth of
the Medway. The official PLA boundary stone lies on the Surrey
bank a few hundred metres downstream of Teddington Lock.
Although the PLA is still with us and, amongst other things,
is responsible for licensing the Society of Thames Mudlarks,
the Thames Conservancy itself was superseded by the Thames
Water Authority in 1974. Its responsibilities then passed via the
National Rivers Authority to the Environment Agency in 1996.

RIVER DREDGING AND DREDGING PROGRAMMES

What river works did these various bodies control? We
have already seen that maintenance of the navigation was
the primary goal of a number of official pronouncements.
Indeed the Minute Books of the City's Committee for
Improving the Navigation of the River Thames and for
Preventing Encroachments Thereon brim with petty
disputes over the 'sloping of rubbish' into the river,
and the breaking down of banks and towpaths by steam
vessels. However, the main method of maintaining the
navigation was dredging, to which we must now turn.

Thames Conservency Dredger
at work near Twickingham, 1883

Traditionally, responsibility for dredging the river upstream of London Bridge rested with the City and later with the Thames Conservancy, downstream it was the responsibility of Trinity House, who monopolised the lucrative right of ballastage in the Pool of London. This curious separation was finally ended in the 1860s when full responsibility for all river dredging was finally vested in the Conservancy.

The quantities (if not quality) of gravel suitable for ship's ballast raised from the Thames downstream of London Bridge were simply prodigious. The total supplied to shipping in 1848 alone was over 615,000 tons, much of which found its way to Newcastle on colliers which had off-loaded cargoes of 'sea-coal' in the capital. It was said to be "really something more than a metaphor to designate this a transfer of the bed of the Thames to the banks of the Tyne." Ballast quays are shown on Hollar's map of the latter river, engraved in 1654, while by the middle of the eighteenth century there were nine huge mounds of ballast at South Shields and a further eighteen between Mill Dam and Jarrow Slake further upstream. Recent excavations conducted near the Sandgate and The Swirle along the Newcastle Quayside, have indicated that the area was levelled up from about the latter part of the thirteenth century using dumped ballast, much of which is of Thames origin.

The traditional speed with which vessels were ballasted in the Pool and the fact that it was often a night-time operation inevitably meant that artefacts must have been missed, and this may, in turn, also explain why there are fewer finds recorded from the reaches downstream of London Bridge. A prehistoric antler-base mattock recovered from Willington Quay on the north bank of the Tyne is thought to have been imported with Thames ballast, while other objects found on or close to the Tyne ballast heaps at South Shields may well have a similar origin.

The absence of detailed dredging records prior to the 1930s makes the location and extent of specific dredging programmes difficult to reconstruct. However, it may be possible to get to grips with this problem by using, for example, the evidence presented to various Parliamentary and Conservancy committees; the reminiscences of dredgermen; dated hydrographic charts, and the concentrations of dated and provenanced finds in museum collections. An initial trawl through the Museum of London's collections has identified a number of relevant pieces.

THE DREDGERMEN

According to Henry Mayhew, writing for the Morning Chronicle in 1849-50, the actual ballasting of the ships in the Pool was undertaken by three classes of labourers: ballast-getters; ballast-lightermen; and ballast-heavers. Mayhew divided ballast-getters into two sub-classes: those who used steam power, and those who still procured it as of old, by muscle power. The steam-dredgers 'Hercules', 'Sampson' and 'Goliath' were at work on the river after 1827 and each was capable of raising up to 4000 tons of ballast a week. By contrast, muscle-power involved the use of a 'spoon and bag', the latter capable of holding up to 20cwt, which required six men to raise it from the riverbed.

Inevitably slower than the steam dredgers, this latter method of ballasting provided greater opportunity for examining the dredged ballast, although, perhaps a trifle naively, Mayhew noted that "the ballast-getters seldom or never fish up anything besides ballast. Four or five years back they were lucky enough to haul up a box of silver plate, but they consider a bit of old iron, or a bit of copper, very good luck now."

Mayhew's second class, ballast-lightermen, were employed to carry the dredged ballast in barges and lighters to the side of the ships requiring stiffening, while his third, ballast-heavers, transferred the ballast from the lighters onto sea-going vessels. A Parliamentary Select Committee Report of 1863 noted that "theirs is among the most laborious toil to which working men can devote themselves." In mid-century none of these ballast men earned much more than around 20 to 25 shillings a week.

OTHER RIVER WORKS:
THE CONSTRUCTION OF NEW LONDON BRIDGE

While dredging was the principal means of maintaining the navigation (and of recovering finds), and one which was carried on virtually non-stop in different reaches of the river, a wide range of other river works was also periodically undertaken. For our purposes these are sometimes more useful sources of information because they are specific as to both time and place, and allow dated and provenanced objects to be related to them. Under this heading we might include the removal of upstanding obstructions such as stakes and old foundations, and the construction and repair of bridges, locks and weirs, towpaths and embankments.

Far and away the most significant were the excavations undertaken for new London Bridge slightly upstream of the old between March 1824 and 1831. These involved the clearing of the riverbed by dredging, and brought up numerous finds. The subsequent removal of the old bridge revealed others, though the foundations remained a hazard to shipping into the 1860s. Antiquary-collectors such as Alfred Kempe, William Knight and John Newman, Comptroller of the Bridge House Estates, were soon on the scene as, a little later, was the celebrated London collector and pioneer archaeologist Charles Roach Smith. Relations between these various individuals were usually cordial if competitive, although Newman and Roach Smith seem to have fallen out over the purchase by the latter of a number of Roman bronzes found in January 1837, which eventually found their way into the British Museum.

Two particular points arise from the London Bridge programme: firstly the recognition by the labourers of the value of the finds they were making, and secondly the realisation of the importance of identifying the destination of the dredgings dumped away from the immediate scene of operations. As regards the first it was noted that "the workmen, who at first considered all the coins they met with as being merely old halfpence, which were worth nothing because they could no longer pass, soon discovered their error, and have now all become connoisseurs."

Regarding the second, we are particularly indebted to the perseverance of Roach Smith who traced the whereabouts of dredgings to the "banks of the Grand Surrey Canal, Deptford"; the riverbank at Battersea; and the towpath between Hammersmith and Barnes and at Putney also. From such localities he retrieved a number of artefacts, while "similar recoveries were made by the aid of juvenile auxiliaries." "Might not some one at a future day say the Romans had a station on this very spot?" Smith mused in his journal, "Not if he sees this record of the fact."

Though massively influential, the London Bridge programme was not alone in furnishing opportunities for the recovery of historic artefacts. Further, if smaller groups of material were obtained, for example, during the renewal or construction of Kingston Bridge (1825–28); Chelsea Bridge (1854–58), and, later in the century, Richmond Lock & Weir (1891–92).

The Chelsea Bridge episode provides a further twist, in that the workmen engaged in its construction, and the dealers to whom they were selling the objects, were particularly anxious not to have their monopoly threatened by divulging the source of their finds. However, they reckoned without the determination of the Walworth antiquary, Henry Syer Cuming. "By dint of vigilant enquiry, and the employment of means which it is not necessary to detail," Cuming soon pinpointed the spot to his own satisfaction, and christened it 'our Celtic Golgotha' because of the numbers of human skulls found there. The famed Battersea shield probably came from this locality, and was sold to the British Museum for the then princely sum of £40 (virtually a year's wages for a ballast-heaver) by a labourer Henry Briggs and one '... Austin'.

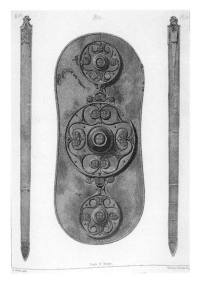

Battersey Shield from Kembel's 'Horae Ferales' of 1863.

Watercolour of the interior of the Old Curiosity Shop as visualised by George Cattermole.

THE CURIOSITY DEALERS

Cuming was to play an equally significant role in unmasking the 'Billies & Charlies' fraud of the late 1850s. This involved the production of hundreds of fake tin-lead objects by two illiterate shore-rakers William Smith and Charles Eaton, who managed to pass them off as genuine medieval antiquities. This enterprise, based in a small workshop on Tower Hill, took in such luminaries as Roach Smith and the Rev Thomas Hugo, the latter a leading light in the newly formed London and Middlesex Archaeological Society.

Whatever other conclusions we may draw from the episode, the role of the dealers William Edwards and George Eastwood, who bought up virtually Billy and Charlie's entire stock, is of particular interest. For such curiosity dealers often acted as middlemen between the labourers and collectors, although as a class they have been little studied hitherto. Some appear to have started out as dealers in shells and other exotic trifles, and can be found listed in various London trade Directories from the 1820s. Dickens provides the following thumbnail sketch of just such an emporium in the first chapter of *The Old Curiosity Shop*, written in weekly installments through 1840–41:

> ... one of those receptacles for old and curious things which seem to crouch in odd corners of this town and hide their misty treasures from the public eye in jealousy and mistrust. There were suits of mail standing like ghosts here and there, fantastic carvings brought from monkish cloisters, rusty weapons of various kinds, distorted figures in china and wood and iron and ivory; tapestry and strange furniture that might have been designed in dreams.

Curiosity dealers were as often as not quite unscrupulous in their dealings, and a thriving trade in forged and falsely provenanced 'London' items soon arose. In an earlier study Geoff Marsh was able to dismiss all of the pieces of early Arretine Ware attributed to City findspots as the result of such activities. Of course the predilections and vanities of individual collectors made them sitting targets for such malpractice; even dealer-collectors such as William Chaffers were themselves duped.

It is one of the minor ironies of London archaeology that Thomas Hugo, one of those taken in by the Billies and Charlies fiasco, had, at just about this time, warned his fellow antiquarians in no uncertain terms against the snares of the market place. In a paper entitled "Frauds of Antiquity Dealers, and Especially the Dealers in So-Called London Antiquities", Hugo railed against "the most shameless and unprincipled imposture" practised on the many enthusiastic London collectors particularly with regard to the attachment of false provenances to otherwise genuine objects. In this way, he continued, "... fragments of pottery from the New Forest and from hundreds of other localities, and whole vessels from the Pan Rock, were brought out of their lurking places, and made to do duty as discoveries in Budge Row and Bush Lane!"

He proffered two pieces of advice: firstly, not to work 'by deputy', but to visit sites personally to make purchases; and, secondly, not to pay over the odds for a particular piece as this encouraged deception. Roach Smith had, twenty years previously, adhered to Hugo's first dictum, even going so far as to row a hired boat out to visit the dredgers in midstream at London Bridge. Thomas Bateman, the Derbyshire antiquary, stuck to the letter of the second by refusing to purchase the base of a bronze cauldron from the river at Battersea "because" as he noted "its owner thought it was a shield and so attached an undue value to it."

THE GENTLEMEN COLLECTORS

We have had much to say about these collectors, but what sort of men were they? (And this being Victorian England, they were all men, though special mention should be made of one intrepid Miss Kincaid who regularly supplied Syer Cuming with antiquities from various City sites in the late 1840s.) Most collectors were, like Cuming, moneyed or professional men, or in trade; they were often Fellows of the Society of Antiquaries of London. Many, like Thomas Layton, were active for decades.

Layton, significantly, was a coal-merchant (bearing in mind the link between sea-coal and ballast-dredging downstream of London Bridge). Others, such as Hugo or William Greenwell of Durham were clerics. William Roots of Kingston and Frank Corner of Poplar were both doctors, Roach Smith a druggist. Augustus Wollaston Franks of the British Museum, Sir John Evans, father of Arthur Evans, and Lord Londesborough, an early patron and President of London and Middlesex Archaeological Society, each had their own private fortunes. William Lloyd junior of St Margaret's near Twickenham, perhaps the least well known of the major London collectors, was the son of a tin packing-case maker, and probably one of the "competitors in Hammersmith and Twickenham" mentioned in a letter from Greenwell to Layton in December 1885. The youthful G F Lawrence may have been another. Interestingly, Lloyd's family owned property just along Brentford High Street from Layton, who lived in a large house on the north side of Kew Bridge.

Greenwell himself was a rapacious, sometimes even unprincipled, collector who hated to be bested in the market place, and a little of his ruthlessness comes across in his austere portrait in Durham Cathedral Library. His collection eventually reached the British Museum through the several offices of Dr Allen Sturge (flints) and J Pierpoint Morgan (metalwork), though he took pains to document and list his purchases in a series of manuscript catalogues happily also in the British Museum. These make it clear that he acquired pieces through a wide circle of agents and acquaintances, both in this country and abroad; many of his London pieces were purchased through Lawrence.

Photograph of Thomas Layton (1819–1911)

Part of the broadness hoard of spearheads dredged drom the Thames in 1892. Courtesy Museum of London.

In an illuminating aside, he was, somewhat unusually, forced to content himself with only a minor portion of the important hoard of spearheads dredged from the river at Broadness in 1892, the larger parts of which were snapped up by Lloyd and Corner. A short spearhead with lunate-openings, pieces of which entered both collections independently, served when re-united to confirm the two groups as part of the same hoard. In his manuscript listing of Lloyd's collection, prepared after the latter's death in 1905, G F Lawrence noted with careful understatement that "Canon Greenwell... thought the find should not have been separated"!

COLLECTIONS AND CONTEXT

The Broadness hoard is, relatively speaking, one of the better recorded groups of material from the river, and in his publication Reginald Smith, using information doubtless supplied to him by Corner, is able to offer a good deal of accompanying contextual information. Close inspection of other collections, both within the Museum of London and beyond, encourages the view that, used judiciously, many have useful information of their own to impart. For example, notations on the artefacts in the small but important collections belonging to William & George Roots record detailed observation of the stratification of the river-bed upstream of Kingston Bridge. These artefacts are now split between the Society of Antiquaries, Kingston Museum and the Ashmolean Museum.

Early Layton material is also tolerably well recorded and like that of the Roots's suggests that he was either present when the objects were found or was on hand to purchase directly from the finder and so ascertain the precise circumstances of discovery. Various hand-written labels mention the relationship between individual finds and "low water," "ferruginous gravel" or "wooden piles" together with their juxtaposition to a local landmark, often a pub, ferry or bridge. One label, stuck on a ground flint axe of Neolithic type, records that the axe was found on the "Bed of Thames off Water Works, Surrey shore, Hammersmith" with "some broken ancient British pottery Feb 1885." Prehistoric pottery recovered from this same stretch is present in a number of collections, including those of Franks and Corner as well as Layton.

It will by now have become clear that it has been possible to touch on only a fraction of the information, riparian, social and archaeological, which exists to document Lawrence's 'Golden Age' of river finds. There has been no time, for instance, to go into the Coway Stakes episode, or to document the antiquarian skirmishing over the precise location of the fortified ford erected against Caesar's advance in 54BC. (This at least was solved, to his own satisfaction, by Montagu Sharpe who placed it at Brentford, and backed it up with, to him, incontrovertible evidence!)

We have, though, already identified, I would suggest, a range of topics with the potential to re-energise study of these historic collections and therefore worthy of further consideration. I would pick out four:

1. the location, reconstruction and study of the dredging records including hydrographic charts, and their comparison with known dated groups of finds

2. the identification of the source and ultimate destination of dredged material (a close and critical inspection of the Tyne & Ware Sites & Monuments Record might prove an interesting starting point)

3. the identity and modus operandi of the curiosity dealers and the contemporary antiquities market

4. detailed studies of the individual collectors and of the contents and contexts of their collections.

This article, an earlier version of which was delivered to the Thames Archaeological Survey Conference in April 1998, represents an initial attempt to review the riparian, social and archaeological background to the great series of finds recovered from the 19th-century Thames.

FURTHER READING

Lawrence, G. F., "Antiquities From the Middle Thames", *Archaeological Journal* 86,1929, pp. 69–98.

Marsh, G., "Nineteenth and Twentieth Century Antiquities Dealers and Arretine Ware from London", *Transactions of the London and Middlesex Archaeological Society* 30,1979, pp. 125–129.

Milne, G., Bates, M. & Webber, M., "Problems, Potential and Partial Solutions: An Archaeological Study of the Tidal Thames", *World Archaeology* 29, 1997, pp. 130–146.

Smith, R., "Bronze Age Hoard Dredged From the Thames Off Broadness", *Proceedings of the Society of Antiquaries of London* 23, 1910, pp. 160–171.

Wainwright, C., *The Romantic Interior: the British Collector at Home 1750–1850*, New Haven: Yale University, 1989.

Whipp, D. & Blackmore, L., "Thomas Layton, FSA (1819–1911). A misguided Antiquary" *London Archaeologist* 3(4), 1977, pp. 90–96.

Wilson, D. M., *The Forgotten Collector: Augustus Wollaston Franks of the British Museum*, London: Thames & Hudson,1984.

ACKNOWLEDGEMENTS

In getting even this far it will be equally apparent that I have benefited from the help and advice of a large number of people, already too numerous to list here. I would, however, like to thank Mark Dion for inviting me to contribute to this volume, and Richard Stroud and Roz Sherris for help with the illustrations. I owe a big thank you too to the staff of the various local studies and museum archives around London whose records I have dipped into and particular thanks to Chris Ellmers and Bob Aspinall at the Museum in Docklands and the PLA Archive. They have been endlessly helpful in making their knowledge and the archives in their care available for study.

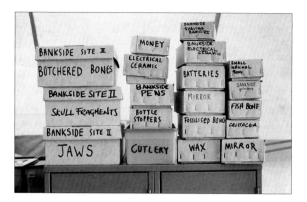

Tate Thames Dig, Site II, detail, 1999.

DISJECTA RELIQUIAE THE TATE THAMES DIG

ROBERT WILLIAMS

The erudition derived from archaeology is far more animated than that we acquire from books.

Madame de Stäel.[1]

Mark Dion's *Tate Thames Dig* has been described as a book with three chapters and an appendix. The three chapters, constituting the activity of the project itself - the collection of material, cleaning & identification of the objects, and their classification and presentation within a cabinet of curiosities, a *Wunderkammer*. The appendix took the form of a series of events and lectures complimentary to the project during the Summer of 1999. However, in taking Madame de Stäel's comment to heart, Dion's *Tate Thames Dig* is not really a book, rather, it is a series of contexts, each of which are associated with the river. Consequently, the project should be viewed as a practice where the process, encompassing the whole range of activities, becomes the artefact. The process is, in itself, analogous to a stratification, it has many different levels to encounter, to explore and to study in each context. The experience of which in its final stage, is as much an archaeological excavation as the methodology and language of the project itself.

"London's Foreshore", *Tate Thames Dig*, 1999. Photo: Andrew Cross.

The context of a dynamic tidal river, its position central to the capital, and carrying as is does material which reflects each epoch of its existence, is undoubtably of significance. The nature of the river as a continuum is reflected in the undifferentiated material that is left on the surface of its banks. Contemporary flotsam and jetsam mingle with objects from all periods, which in a sense, confounds and challenges archaeological method, in that it is impossible to recognise a true stratigraphy. Even if the foreshore is considered to be an horizon, this co-existence of objects defies easy categorisation. A state of democratic 'timelessness' exists in the assemblage, all objects are equally subjected to the vicissitudes of the river. Even though it is possible to establish a chronology for the objects that have been found on an individual basis, using typology, laboratory based dating techniques, and other archaeological methods; the question remains as to what value such data would have for the project? Perhaps it is more appropriate to view the River as a structure, with the finds acting as evidence of its nature and character. The Thames also has its own cultural history, undeniably bound to the city, and carrying meaning within its waters – whether as an economic resource for the earliest inhabitants of London, a sacred site into which votive offerings were made, a mercantile resource, a means of transportation and communication, an aesthetic icon, and as a conduit for urban waste.

The river, then, is an iconographic artefact in its own right, one that has long been of value to history and archaeology – the Museum of London, and the British Museum, house a vast number of objects recovered from its banks. The early Antiquarians were well aware of the potential for finds – as were mudlarkers and workmen in the late 1880s, who were not beyond the fabrication of false antiquities to feed the acquisitive demand from collectors.[2] The Thames, as much as Dion's vitrine, can be considered to be a museum, containing a collection of material finding its way into the river, where it is sorted and classified according to the river's own internal physical dynamics, those of transport and deposition, tide, current and flow.

It is appropriate then, that an artist wishing to explore issues of archaeology, should choose to investigate the material remains of the past, and the implications of this for the present on a multiplicity of levels, to make this river the subject of his enquiry. Appropriate too, is Dion's strategy to use aspects of archaeological method (past and contemporary), as a mirror in which its models and practices are reflected.

"Mark Dion beachcombing on London's Foreshore", *Tate Thames Dig*, Site I, 1999. Photo: Andrew Cross.

PHASE 1 – COLLECTING METHODOLOGY

It is said of Antiquaries, they wipe off the mouldinesse they digge, and remove the rubbish.
— John Aubrey (1670)[3]

The collecting methodology for the first phase of the project was straightforward, and followed the established practice of fieldwalking in order to identify surface finds. Within archaeological method, this is usually as a prelude to either a more detailed survey, or excavation; however in this case, the practice became the principle activity for the collection of objects, and reflected the conditions of the River, given that material occurred as a scatter, rather than a stratigraphy. Consequently, the two sites at Millbank and Bankside were selected, and all searching activity took place within identified boundaries. Permission was sought and granted from the Port of London Authority for the gathering to take place. This was agreed on the proviso that no digging below a depth of six inches would be allowed, principally in order to avoid any ecological disturbance in what is now a conservation area.

"London's Foreshore – Detail",
Tate Thames Dig, 1999.

Prior to, and during the collecting phase of the project, and in line with current archaeological practice, advice was sought from specialists in a wide variety of different disciplines. Information was gathered from the Thames River Police, from ecologists monitoring the health of the River, historians who could offer insights into past uses of the sites, and from archaeologists. In short, Dion, and the volunteers were well appraised of the environment for their activity, and prepared to be open minded about what they might find. This is an important point to make in view of the instructions for fieldwalking. Dion's brief to the volunteer field work team asked them to adopt what he calls a "scatter-gun" approach, to identify and collect anything that caught their attention – chasing the anomaly in the best tradition of classic archaeological method. In this sense a democratic/collaborative process was reinforced, in that the act of collection reflected the individual faculties and interests of twenty five different people.[4] In microcosm, this is a dynamic with a long history, antiquaries and early archaeologists gathered that which particularly interested them. The acquisitive impulse itself, has been the motor which has driven archaeology in its most fundamental form.

"Beachcombing on London's Foreshore", *Tate Thames Dig*, Site I, 1999. (Previous page). Photo: Andrew Cross.

Mark Dion: *Tate Thames Dig*, 1999.

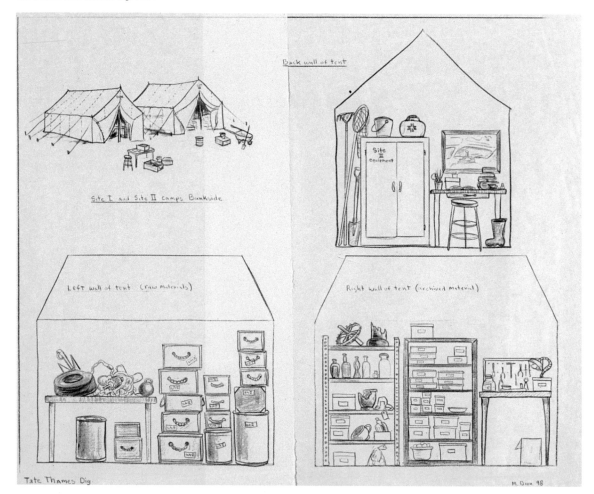

Because of the tidal patterns of the River, collecting could only take place during two hour time slots. Similarly, collecting times varied from early in the morning to late evening over the two week period of the 'dig'. The conditions at each of the sites varied enormously, both in frequency and nature of found material, as well as in the changing landscape of the riverbank after each tide. Site I at Millbank was perhaps the more problematic, with a deep layer of thick, stinking silt often coating and obscuring surface material, making collecting a difficult process. The action of the tide, in obliterating traces of the previous days material, was particularly violent. Here, there was a preponderance of plastic objects, relatively recent pottery, and quantities of metal. Of the more sinister finds reported by Lenka Clayton, were a series of knives, and blank firearm rounds found just below the new MI6 headquarters. Nevertheless, *Tate Thames Dig* staples, clay pipes, glass bottle fragments, and plastic objects, also appeared in abundance.

The Bankside site in contrast, was a much calmer environment, an area where the river could reduce speed, and deposit many of the objects it had carried thus far. This allowed an opportunity for a somewhat less frenetic pattern of collecting; and whilst the site yielded much more material, it was possible to seek further anomalies within the assemblage. The condition of the pottery fragments at Bankside, also revealed a much greater passivity in the action of the river, suggesting that material deposited at the site had remained there over time. Millbank finds were often very small and fragmented, whilst Bankside ceramic pieces were found to be larger, some vessels and plates remaining intact. Bankside provided huge numbers of bones and oyster shells – perhaps reflecting its history as the entertainment centre for seventeenth and eighteenth century London, with it's chop-houses and 'stews' catering to a clientele hungry for all manner of flesh.

PHASE 2 – ORGANISATION IN THE FIELD – THE FIELD CENTRE.

Field-work takes the student-collector into the open air to some
of the wildest portions of the country, where he can conveniently
combine with the study of prehistoric archaeology, the pursuit
of geology, ornithology, botany, entomology, conchology, or
branches of natural history....
– W.G. Clarke (1922)[6]

Following the arduous task of gathering vast amounts of
material, the next phase of the project was to clean, identify and
organise the finds. The tents established on the South Lawn of
the Tate, hitherto used to store the unsorted boxes of material,
now became the field centre for sorting and analysis. The
procedure for cleaning and identifying the material also followed
broad archaeological method in dealing with finds, and advice
had been taken from Professor Colin Renfrew, and Museum
of London staff, amongst others. The field centre was well
equipped with storage furniture, and work benches, complete
with lights, at which finds could be worked on.
Tent A, was set up as an interpretation centre to document
progress of the project. This was available for public use, and
contained a vitrine for the display of individual finds (archaeologists
would be familiar with the term "small finds"), a timetable
of events, maps identifying the collection sites, together with
a series of photographs showing the collecting in progress at
each of the sites.

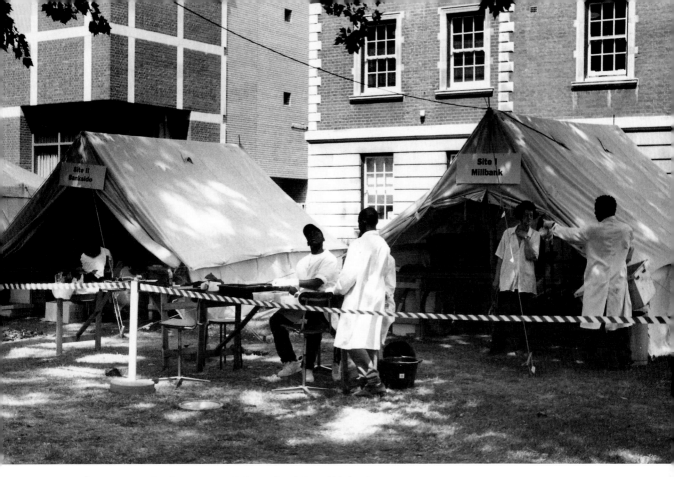

Mark Dion: "Millbank Site", *Tate Thames Dig*, 1999. Photo: Tate Gallery of Modern Art.

Each field worker on a particular shift would take an unsorted box of finds, the material would then be cleaned of all mud and debris during washing. The majority of finds were robust enough to be cleaned using small brushes and scourers. Objects were sorted into categories, and left to dry. Great care was taken not to confuse material from the different sites. As field workers sorted finds into broad categories – ceramic, glass, bone, leather, shells, organic, plastic, metal, and so on, Dion and the field centre managers set about organising the different 'species' of objects according to sub-divisions largely suggested by a typography of objects (see list of finds in appendix). This developed taxonomy of objects would later inform the basis for the design, and organisation of the Cabinet. At this stage, Dion examined the material, identifying items of particular interest – some of which were placed in the small vitrine in Tent A for the duration of the field centre phase. The majority of finds were deposited in labelled category boxes in either of the site tents, as a prelude to their organisation within the Cabinet.

Whilst a labour intensive task, this activity was also very compelling. Field workers discussed and compared objects, and indulged in speculation as to the nature of the finds as they emerged from the obscuring mud. Similarly, the more 'spectacular' finds that came to light, occasioned a good deal of excitement for all involved. Amongst these included two messages in bottles – one in Arabic, carefully restored by the Tate's Paper Conservation Department; and another in Italian, translated by Tate staff to be a wistful, homesick love letter from a schoolgirl on a study trip to London. Equally exciting were the shards of Ballarmine pottery, or 'Greybeards', originally stoneware jugs made in Germany during the late seventeenth century, and often used as 'witch bottles' for magical charms or curses.[7] Other shards of Mediaeval and Elizabethan pottery were also tentatively identified amongst the great mass of nineteenth century ceramic. Amongst the bones from the Bankside site were mostly those of butchered food animals – cattle, sheep, pig (as evidenced by butchery marks), and horse. There were also a number of very heavy, possibly fossilised bones, as well as the only human fragment found – a damaged and very weathered tibia or shinbone.

The democratic nature of the collection, provides us with a microcosmic slice of both natural, and human activity on the banks of the Thames. Given that all the objects discovered on the digs, and later during sorting, were deemed equally important. The collection at this stage represented a broad sample of material deposited by the River over a huge span of time; from the fossilised sea-urchin test from the Eocene period, some 50 million years old; to the green, bendy toy alien and lost mobile cellphone of 1999 – and all that lies in between.

PHASE 3 – CONSEQUENCES

Archaeology is the latest born of the sciences. It has but
scarcely struggled into freedom, out of the swaddling clothes
of dilettante speculations. It is still attached to pretty things,
rather than by real knowledge. It has to find shelter with the
Fine Arts or with History, and not a single home has yet been
provided for its real growth.
— W.M. Flinders-Petrie (1904)[8]

Increasingly, current archaeology as a practice has adopted
similar philosophical frameworks which are applied to art
as a practice. Indeed, as Flinders-Petrie's rhetorical statement
suggests, the relationship between art and archaeology has
been present since the early days. The emphasis on the
empirical aspirations of archaeology (no less an issue for
Modernist Art of the same period) which has informed method,
practice and paradigm, has served to make a distance between
the two on ideological grounds.

Postmodern and post-processual theories within contemporary archaeological thought is clearly explained by Professor Colin Renfrew, as revolutionary new dimensions in the consideration of the products of archaeology.[9] The development of this into an hermeneutic framework, as he observes, is one which emphasises a diversity of approaches, and whilst opposing generalisation, recognises a multiplicity of interpretations on many different levels. However, this is not a particularly revolutionary concept within recent and contemporary art, either within practice, or as a model for criticism. Rather than remaining fixed in theory, art has – certainly in the twentieth century – functioned to question, and to challenge canonical thought, even as theories emerged to account for the art. Granted, that this has not occurred without reference to the infrastructure of art or culture; context within art history and theory is just as important as context in archaeology for an explanation of this as a phenomenon. Nevertheless, the centrality of interpretation recognises many levels of meaning. Necessarily, this involves the evolution of strategies for the evocation of different paradigms, and different agendas. Whilst applied to the specific object (artwork and artefact) or association of objects (the collection/exhibition or assemblage), an interpretive model such as this, can be regarded as a bridge which links, in this case, contemporary art and archaeology as epistemological study. Particularly so in Mark Dion's project, where the role of the museum, of the collection itself and the narratives that are constructed by collections, are raised as issues to be considered as a consequence of the models, methodology and practice of the project.

It may be a truism that any given collection (in whatever form) provides as much of an insight into the agenda of the collector, as it does of the material itself. This is not difficult to demonstrate if we consider examples such as the Pitt-Rivers Museum, or the Cuming Museum, The British Museum, and even the Tate itself. In each case, the ideology, expectations, and world view of the 'curator' is manifested. For Dion, whilst acknowledging, and indeed taking part in the debate about the politics, culture, and psychology of the museum, he argues that such collections should remain intact, rather than constantly modified and used to create different narratives. It is the world view of the collector which should be preserved. The real value – in educational, scientific, artistic and theoretical terms, should be in witnessing, and participating in the process of collection and analysis. Dion calls for the display areas of museums to ossify, whilst the field-centres, laboratories, workshops, store rooms and studios should be opened. In a sense, this is what he has done with the *Tate Thames Dig* project.[10]

The *Tate Thames Dig* has been what Dion may call a "site oriented" project (as distinct from a site-specificity, which implies a different set of concerns). The 'place' – physically, socially, and culturally, is significant in his consideration of the strategies and methodologies for practice that he has employed; from the identification of the collection boundaries, the advice sought from individuals familiar with the area, to the involvement of contemporary Southwark residents as field workers. The collaborative aspects of the project function to reinforce this, whilst at the same time address the issues of the authoritative institutional framework. In practice, the role of the volunteer field workers has been considerable in forming, and forwarding the project. True, that Dion is undoubtably the originator and director of the project, it is nevertheless significant that he is not the sole 'collector'.

Mark Dion: "Bankside Site – Detail", *Tate Thames Dig*, 1999. Photo: Lenka Clayton.

Similarly, the field workers contribution has been more than to be mere providers of labour, in the manner of the navvies used by nineteenth century barrow diggers, particularly in the identification and collection of material from the digs. They have been participants in the categorisation of objects during the different phases, as well as in the discourse, interpretation, and presentation of the project as a whole. The volunteers have another, equally important role – that of representatives of the locality, the site itself. As contemporary inhabitants of Southwark, living alongside the Thames, they are a link with those of the past, whose flotsam and jetsam they have been collecting. The relationship between people and the continuum of the river is reinforced through their participation in the project.

The *Tate Thames Dig*, rather than being art 'playing' at archaeology, is in practice both art and archaeology in all their respective aspects. The project carries with it the values and expectations of interpretation for both disciplines, and perhaps reveals much more about their similarities, than it does their differences. Changed and challenged also, are our preconceptions of either discipline, their application and presence within the museum as authoritative, structural, aesthetic and interpretive frameworks. Both in terms of practice in the field, and the preserving of its products within a museum. The consequence of either activity, is to present interpretable objects which exist in a state of hermeneutic flux, which while they themselves remain physical realities, are nevertheless open to broader debate and consideration. In turn, this alters their relative and associative significance, and consequently the manner in which they are experienced from context to context, and age to age.

Mark Dion: "Detail", *Tate Thames Dig*, 1999. Photo: Lenka Clayton.

This can be demonstrated using examples from the field, the reading of which recognises the significance of temporally undifferentiated material becoming associated with each other, the site acting as the linking factor. By allowing this, rather than a chronology, to influence interpretation, a different space can be opened which suggests new areas for exploration. At Bankside, several pages from a paperback book were found. The only readable portion of text was a poem by the classical lyric poet, Catullus. Bearing in mind that this part of Southwark was, during the seventeenth and eighteenth centuries, the venal capital of London, it is interesting to note that Catullus's poem can be read as a satirical ode to the erection:

> Naso! An elevated personage
> With a stoop, however, bespeaking
> a somewhat different sort of 'elevation'.
> Indeed an elevated person.

— Gaius Valerius Catullus Poem 11211

In some way, a linkage has been made between a Roman poet, famous for the 'obscene' nature of his writing, who died in 54BC; an area of London famed for its decadence and fleshly pleasures, the evidence for which exists in historical sources, supported by material from the dig itself (bones and oyster shells); and a poem printed on the page of a paperback book at some point during the last decade. Even though archaeological methods could establish that there is no actual dating evidence for their connection, it cannot dispute that an association exists, or that the association is meaningful within the context of the dig. What is needed here, in order to account for this (coincidence can be meaningful too) is, perhaps, a re-framing of the purpose for their collection; which after all, is one of the issues that Dion's project raises. This application of what may be considered by archaeologists to be an extreme of post-precessual method, might in this case, reveal something that could, and should be explored. A space has been created, allowing for a different construction of what may be significant in these circumstances, relative to objects found in association with each other. Clearly, a certain amount of prior knowledge must exist for this connection to take place, but is this not also part of the archaeological model?

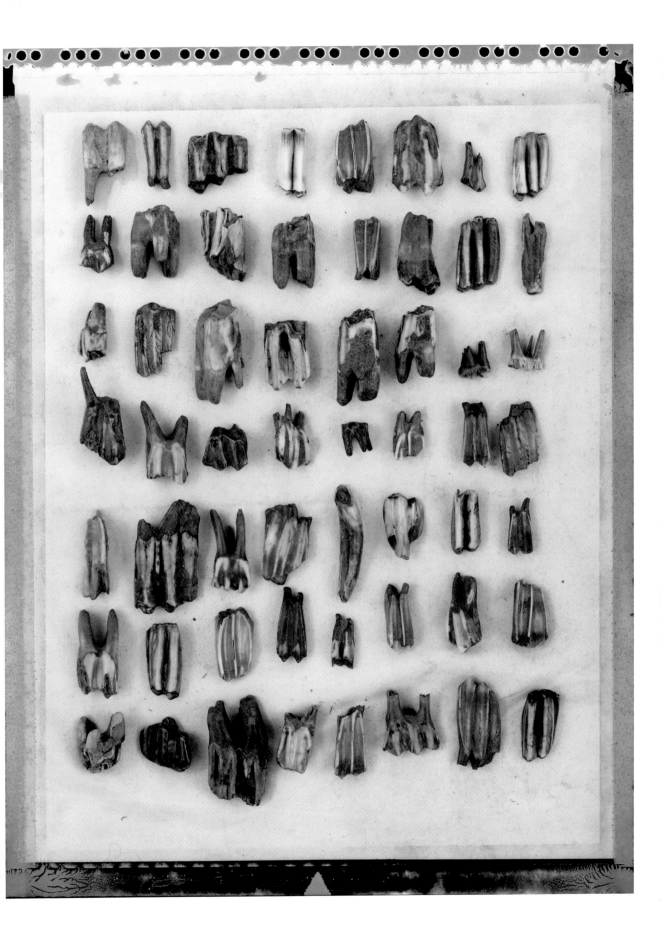

Naomi Beckwith
Field Centre Manager

Lenka Clayton
Field Centre Manager

Mark Dion
Artist

Robert Foot
Dig Team

Adrian George
Publicity Department

Bego Garcia
Camera Crew

Joan Godfrey
Dig Team

Alexis Holley
Dig Team

Caro Howell
Education Department

Abdul Jalloh
Dig Team

Mandy Kowalewski
Dig Team

Gulcan Mahmut
Dig Team

Steve Mallaghan
Film Crew

Fahima Matin
Dig Team

Sophie McKinlay
Curator

Sira Meinerikandathevan
Dig Team

Phil Monk
Project Manager

Frances Morris
Curator

Beatrice Oluwa
Dig Team

Mark Dion:
Tate Thames Dig,
Tate Gallery of
Modern Art, 1999.
Photos: A. Dunkley

Ruth Owogemi
Dig Team

Jerome Perrins
Dig Team

Kelly Pratt
Dig Team

Denise Ramzy
Education Department

David Reez
Camera Crew

Hamsini Satchithanthan
Dig Team

Carmen Servais
Dig Team

Stacey Smith
Dig Team

THE WUNDERKAMMER

Moreover, Archaeology is not only a study of curiosity and
instruction, but is highly auxiliary to taste.
— The Rev. Thomas Dudley Fosbroke. MA FSA. London (1840)[12]

At the conclusion of the first two phases of the project, we are
left with a museum of objects that will remain intact, and which
satisfies Dion's fantasy to preserve the collection. The four
metre long, double sided cabinet housing the accumulated
objects from the Tate Thames Dig, itself makes reference to
nineteenth century display furniture. It is modeled on classic
display cases such as those to be seen in, for example, the
Pitt-Rivers Museum, or the Museum of Natural History, or any
other great Victorian museum. Unlike its forebears however,
Dion's Wunderkammer is meant to be interactive, viewers
are invited to browse, and to excavate its contents. There is
no labeling, no chronology, and no interpretive text other than
a reference to the sites where the material was gathered; in
this the Tate Thames Dig Wunderkammer encapsulates the
process of its formation. Not only in terms of the individual
objects held within it, but also in the manner of their gathering,
and the establishment of relationships and associations
between objects, which undoubtably affects their reading
and interpretation. This is the space within which the audience
is invited to participate in their consideration of the objects,
the collection and the setting that they encounter. It is wholly
appropriate then, that we find the Cabinet within the Art Now
Room of the Tate Gallery of Modern Art, despite the fact that
it speaks with the voice of the past, it articulates the language
of the present.

Mark Dion: "Wunderkammer", *Tate Thames Dig*, 1999.

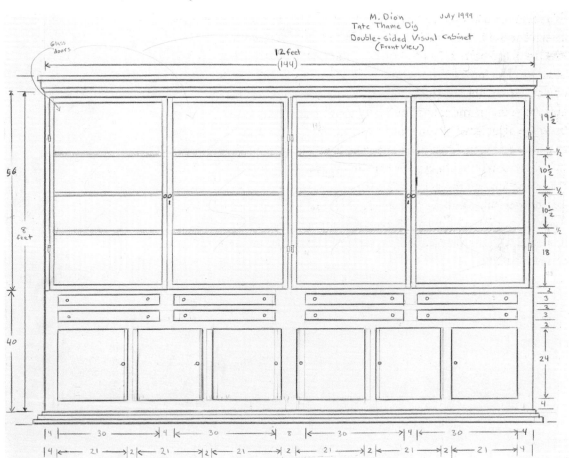

NOTES TO THE TEXT

1 Quoted in Nichols, John Bowyer, *Fosbroke's Encyclopaedia of Antiquities*, London, 1840, p. 1.

2 See Jessup, R., "False Antiquities", *The Story of Archaeology in Britain*, London: Michael Joseph,1964, p. 130.

3 Quoted in Cleator, P. E. , "Archaeology Defined", *Archaeology in the Making*, London: Hale, 1976, p. 13.

4 "One of the aims of the Tate Thames Dig was to involve volunteers from the local community as a way to introduce the Tate Gallery of Modern art to Southwark and the surrounding area. Local community groups and schools were contacted about the project and invited to a preliminary meeting with the artist, Mark Dion, at Bankside. The project was also advertised in the local press. When the site moved to Millbank students involved in TateExtra, an afterschool programme at the Tate, got involved. The team consists mainly of youth and some seniors. They live primarily in South London and learned about the *Tate Thames Dig* from groups including Blackfriars Settlement, Union of Youth, St. Giles Trust Day Centre, Southwark Youth service and local schools." Press release from The Tate Gallery Marketing Office. 1999.

5 Dion is in mind of Pitt-Rivers's statements concerning field work method, and its role in creating collections eg:"Excavators, as a rule, record only those things which appear to them to be important at the time, but fresh problems in Archaeology and Anthropology are constantly arising, and it can hardly fail to have escaped the notice of anthropologists, especially those, who like myself, have been concerned with the morphology of art, that on turning back to old accounts in search of evidence, the points which would have been most valuable have been passed over from being thought uninteresting at the time. Every detail should, therefore, be recorded in the manner most conducive to facility of reference, and it ought at all times to be the chief object of an excavator to reduce his own personal equation to a minimum." Pitt-Rivers quoted in Brian, Fagan, (ed), "Revolutionizing Excavation", *Eyewitness to Discovery*, Oxford: Oxford Univeristy Press, , 1996, p. 394.

6 Clarke, W.G., "The Pleasures of Fieldwork", *Our Homeland Prehistoric Antiquities & How to Study Them*, London: Homeland Association , 1922, p. 118.

7 For a fascinating discussion of Witch Bottles see: Merrifield, R., "Charms Against Witchcraft", *The Archaeology of Ritual and Magic*, London: Guild, 1987, p. 163.

8 Cleator, *Archaeology*, p. 114.

9 Renfrew, C. and P. Bahn, *Archaeology: Theories, Methods and Practice*, London: Thames & Hudson, 1998.

10 "When it comes to museums, I'm an ultra-conservative. To me the museum embodies the 'official story' of a particular group of people. It is a time capsule. So I think once a museum is opened, it should remain unchanged as a window into the obsessions and prejudices of a period, like the Pitt-Rivers in Oxford, the Museum of Comparative Anatomy in Paris and the Teyler Museum in Haarlem. If someone wants to update the museum, they should build a new one. An entire city of museums would be nice, each stuck in its own time.... So I say freeze the museum's front rooms as a time capsule and open up the laboratories and storerooms to reveal art and science as the dynamic processes they are." Mark Dion quoted in interview with Miwon Kwon, *Mark Dion*, London: Phaidon, 1997, pp. 17–19.

11 P. Wigham, (trans.) Poem Number 112, *The Poems of Catullus*, Harmondsworth: Penguin, 1966–1988, p. 224.

12 Nichols, *Encyclopaedia*, p. vii.

Mark Dion: *Tate Thames Dig*, large nail and Dutch smoked salmon enamel sign, 1999.

APPENDIX 1
Schematic of Collection Methodology

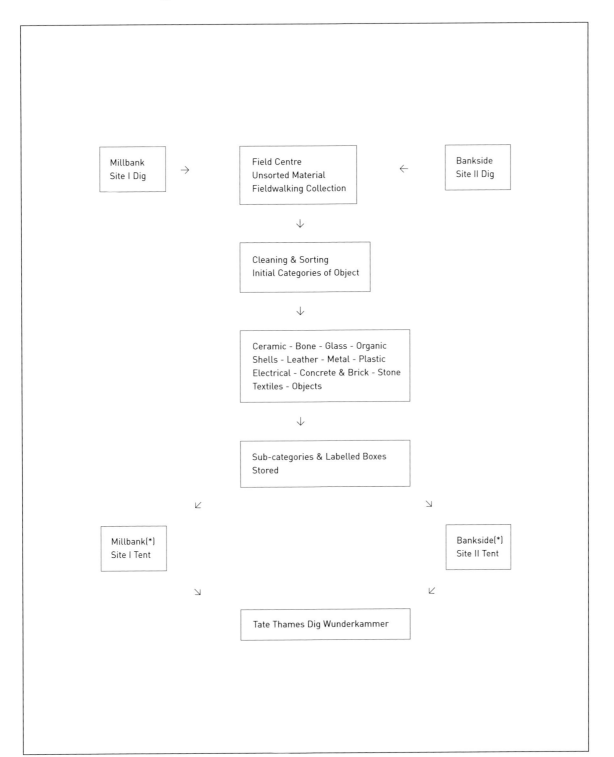

Mark Dion: *Tate Thames Dig*, selection of metal buttons, 1999.

Mark Dion: *Tate Thames Dig*, two clay pipes, 1999.

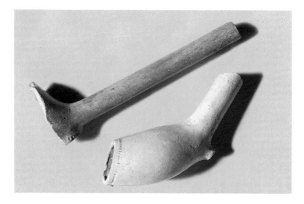

Mark Dion: *Tate Thames Dig*, pineapple fridge magnet, 1999.

CERAMIC	BONE	GLASS	ORGANIC
Decorated Blue & White Earthenware	Large Mammal	Fragments - Clear	Crustacea
Decorated - Colours Earthenware	Small Mammal	Fragments - Green	Feathers
Plain White Earthenware	Bird	Fragments - Brown	Seeds
Brown Stoneware		Fragments - White	Fruit
Beige Stoneware		Fragments - Blue	Preserved:
Clay Pipes		Fragments - Patterned	Marine Alge
Tiles		Fragments - Decorated	Fish
Mosaic		Fragments - Text	Crustacea
Drain pipe		Bottle Necks	Mollusc
Brick		Whole Bottles	Coconut
		Mirror	
		Marbles	

SHELLS	WOOD	LEATHER	METAL
Freshwater Bivalve	Cork	Fragments - Shoes	Nails
Marine Bivalve	Fragments	Whole Shoes	Pins
Freshwater Mollusc		Whole Belts	Long/Straight
Marine Mollusc			Bottle Tops
Land Mollusc			Chain
			Concretions
			Fragments
			Cable
			Keys

PLASTIC	ELECTRICAL	TEXTILES	CONCRETE
Bottles	Circuits	Natural	Fragments
Bottle Tops	Radio	Synthetic	
Safety Helmets	Battery cells	Boot Laces	
Combs & Brushes	Bulbs	Hairties	
Toys	Speakers	Gloves	
Cutlery	Telephones	Socks	
Pens		Rope	
Credit Cards			
Lighters			
Fragments			

TOOLS	STONE	INDIVIDUAL OBJECTS	BOX 001
Grinders	Flint Pebbles	Message in a Bottle:	Unidentified
Trowel	Building Stone	Arabic (restored)	
Screwdriver	Slate	Italian (translated)	
		Bullets	

Mark Dion: *Tate Thames Dig*, large nail and tooth, 1999.

Mark Dion: *Tate Thames Dig*, ceramic lions head and thimble, 1999.

CERAMIC	BONE	GLASS	ORGANIC
Decorated Blue & White	Large Mammal	Fragments - Clear	Crustacea
Earthenware	Small Mammal	Fragments - Green	Feathers
Decorated - Colours	Jaw Bones	Fragments - Brown	Seeds
Earthenware	Teeth	Fragments - White	Fruit
Plain White	Skull Fragments	Fragments - Blue	Coconut
Earthenware	Human Tibia	Fragments - Patterned Wax	
Brown Stoneware	Fish	Fragments - Decorated	
Beige Stoneware	Butchery Marks	Fragments - Text	
Clay Pipes		Bottle Necks	
Tiles		Whole Bottles	
Mosaic		Bottle Bases	
Whole Cups		Drinking Glasses	
Whole Plates		Bottle Stoppers	
Staffordshire Slipware			
Buttons			
Brick			

SHELLS	WOOD	LEATHER	METAL
Freshwater Bivalve	Natural	Fragments - Shoes	Nails
Marine Bivalve	Machined	Whole Shoes	Money
Freshwater Mollusc	Objects	Whole Belts	Long/Straight
Marine Mollusc		Objects (bucket handle)	Bottle Tops
Land Mollusc			Toys
			Concretions
			Fragments:
			Large.
			Small.
			Cutlery.
			Buttons

PLASTIC	ELECTRICAL	TEXTILES	CONCRETE
Bottles	Circuits	Natural	Fragments
Bottle Tops	Radio	Synthetic	
Safety Helmets	Battery cells	Carpet	
Combs & Brushes	Bulbs	Handles/straps	
Toys	Wire/Cable	Zips	
Cutlery	Telephones	Rope	
Pens	Electrical Ceramic		
Razors			
Lighters			
Audio Tapes			
Dummies			
Watches			

Tools	Stone	Individual Objects	Box 001
Various	Flint Pebbles	Wax Figure	Unidentified
	Fossil Echinoderm		
	Fossil Bone		

Thursday 8 July
A tour of Millbank Penitentiary (destroyed 1890s)
Krzysztof Cieszkowski, Acquisitions Librarian,
Tate Gallery

Tuesday 13 July
Toil, Glitter, Grime & Wealth on a Flowing Tide:
Shipping Life on the River Thames
Jack Warrens, Head Paintings Conservation Technician,
Tate Gallery

Wednesday 14 July
From Houses of Ill Repute to Palaces of Art:
Bankside from the Sixteenth Century
Richard Humphreys, Head of Interpretation & Education,
Tate Gallery of British Art

Thursday 15 July
The Curious Collection of Richard & Henry Cuming:
Southwark's History told through Finds, Fakes and
Forgeries Keith Bonnick, Museum Officer, Cuming Museum

Monday 19 July
The Wildlife of the Thames
Alison Taylor, Trust Officer, Thames Explorer Trust

Tuesday 20 July
Archaeology, Interpretation and Art:
The Status of the Discovered Object
Professor Colin Renfrew (Lord Renfrew of Kainsthorn),
MacDonald Institute of Archaeological Research

Wednesday 21 July
The Port of London: The History of London as a
Port from the Eighteenth Century
Alex Werner, Curator of Social & Working History,
Museum of London

Tuesday 27 July
A Mart of Many Nations: London's Diverse
Population from Prehistoric Times to the Present
Dr Nick Merriman, Senior Lecturer,
Institute of Archaeology

Thursday 29 July
Ballast-Heavers and Battle-axes:
The Golden Age of Thames Finds
John Cotton, Curator Pre-History,
Museum of London

Thursday 29 July
The Port of Roman London: Discovering London's First
Harbour Gustav Milne, Lecturer in London Archaeology,
University College London

Monday 2 August
Field Trip: Museum of London
Helen Ganaris, Senior Conservator Archaeology

Tuesday 3 August
PC Steve Davies: The History and Work of the Thames Division
PC Steve Davies, Metropolitan Police Thames Division

Wednesday 4 August
Tales from the Riverbank:
The Thames as a Site of Contemporary Art
Helena Blaker, artist

Field Trip:
Peter Blake's Studio

Thursday 5 August
The History of London's Riverside Entertainments
Patrick Spottiswoode, Head of Education, Globe Theatre

Tuesday 10 August
London's Ice Ages: The Thames Frost Fairs
Jeremy Smith, Guildhall Library

Wednesday 11 August
Thames Living History: Archaeology & Environment on the
Thames
Mike Webber, Curator Thames Living History, Museum of
London

Notes on the Contributers

Alex Coles is founding editor of *de-, dis-, ex-.* (Black Dog Publishing Limited) and co-author of *Walter Benjamin for Beginners*. He is currently undertaking PhD research at Goldsmith's College where he is also a visiting lecturer.

Jonathan Cotton is Curator of Prehistory at the Museum of London, and has a long-standing interest in the collections of objects dredged from the Thames River in the nineteenth century.

Emi Fontana is director of Galleria Emi Fontana, Milan.

Colin Renfrew is Professor of Archaeology at the University of Cambridge and the author of *Before Civilisation: The Radiocarbon Revolution and Prehistoric Europe*, *Archaeology and Language: The Puzzle of Indo-European Origins* and (with Paul Bahn) *Archaeology: Theories, Methods and Practice*.

Robert Williams is a visual artist and Course Leader in Fine Art at Cumbria College of Art and Design, Carlisle. He worked closely with Mark Dion on the Storey Tasting Garden in Lancaster and was an active participant in the Tate Thames Dig.

Colophon

© 1999 Black Dog Publishing Limited, the artist, authors and photographers.

All opinions expressed in material contained within this publication are those
of the author and not necessarily those of the publisher.

No part of this publication may be reproduced, stored in a retrieval system,
or transmitted, in any form or by any means, electronic, mechanical, photocopying,
recording, or otherwise, without the prior permission of the publisher.

Edited by Alex Coles and Mark Dion
Produced by Duncan McCorquodale
Designed by Christian Küsters

Printed in the European Union.

ISBN 1 901033 91 0

British Library cataloguing-in-publication data.
A catalogue record of this book is available from
The British Library.

Cover photo by Andrew Cross.